D0204401

Surviving a Sibling

Discovering Life After Loss

Scott Mastley

I

ISBN 0-9702369-0-5

Printed in the United States of America
The Box Press

What People Are Saying About <u>Surviving a Sibling</u>

"<u>Surviving a Sibling</u> is a much needed resource written by a bereaved sibling. It deals head-on with questions that we all have after ...one of the greatest losses of our lives."
– *Daniel Yoffee. National Sibling Representative, The Compassionate Friends*

"You'll never know how many lives you have touched by writing this. Finally, someone who really understands what it's like to lose a brother or a sister."
– *Lisa Jaspersohn. Surviving Sibling*

"Simple eloquence."
– *Letitia Sweitzer. The Village Writer's Group*

"Sibling grief is so different from a parent's grief. My daughter and I recognize the differences and respect each other's loss, but most of society does not. If you have a surviving sibling, I highly recommend purchasing one of these books. It will be helpful to both you and your children. It is an easy reading book that speaks from the heart."
– *Jayne Newton. Bereaved Parent and Newsletter/Website Editor for the Tucker Chapter of TCF*

"<u>Surviving a Sibling</u> is a must read for those whose sibling died from an accident or died suddenly from any cause, but all of us bereaved siblings will appreciate the new perspective Scott brings to the understanding of grief. Thank you, Scott, for sharing your brother and your story with us."
– *Pleasant Gill White, Ph.D. The Sibling Connection*

"I have finished your book and I can truthfully say it has brought me more comfort and peace than any I have read."
– *Martha Grogan. Surviving Sibling*

"My loss as a parent is horrible, but I know there are things a sibling feels that I can't even begin to address. Thank you for your wonderful book and for sharing those things that only a sibling can understand!"
– *Peggy Orr. Bereaved Parent*

"I believe that it is one of the most powerful books that I have ever read."
– *Kitty Byers*

"It is absolutely a marvelous book."
– *Carlton Joyce, Author of <u>Stand Where They Fought</u>*

In memory of my brother, Chris, whose life reached out to those around him and warmed them like rays of the sun.

For surviving siblings.

ACKNOWLEDGEMENTS

I would like to thank Jim Dirr for showing up every month at The Compassionate Friends' meetings to help me and countless others learn to live with our grief. Thank God for The Compassionate Friends! I am grateful to Charlie Walton and Dennis Linnekin for reading the early drafts of the manuscript and for giving me sound advice and encouragement. I am indebted to Letitia Sweitzer, who edited several drafts of the book, kept me high on her priority list for months, and provided solid guidance along the way. My deepest gratitude goes to Nancy Fox for sharing her expertise and to Christiane C. O'Hara for her suggestions, her Introduction, and her years of friendship. Thanks to Ellis Loyd for helping me keep my message clear and for choosing to be a teacher; I never learned more about writing than when I was in his class in high school. I appreciate Michelle Lombardo's help with formatting, Mark Herron's cover artwork and Holly Painter's photograph of the author. I was fortunate to benefit from the many survey participants who took the time to invest emotionally in this process by answering personal questions about their grief, and I appreciate their input.

My parents taught me to be a good person and to excel, and they taught me to live and love fully. My appreciation for their sacrifices and family focus grows daily. My wife, Doreen, and baby girl, Molly, have given me the opportunity to both demonstrate and receive the kind of love I was taught to admire. Doreen has been supportive and understanding throughout this process, and I am fortunate to be married to someone who maintains such enthusiasm for the things I hold dear to my heart.

Table of Contents

Introduction by Christiane C. O'Hara, Ph.D.

My older brother and I had a relationship that friends and teachers described as enviable. We learned sports together as children and discovered girls at about the same time. In high school Chris cheered emotionally for me at all of my wrestling matches, and I encouraged his play on the soccer field. In college we joined the same fraternity, and after college we both moved back to Atlanta to work and look for a house. He was going to buy it, and I was going to rent a room from him. Our future plans were laid. The day I got the call that Chris was killed in a car accident, I just couldn't believe it. The world kept spinning, and my brother had to leave it. I was jolted out of my peaceful existence into a daily struggle to live a positive life. My world became a world of grief, and I had to learn to survive. Even today I lose him every day, every time I remember.

Surviving siblings are treated differently than bereaved parents. Friends and relatives express their sympathy for the parents but do not recognize the grief of surviving siblings. Surviving siblings become sympathy messengers, relaying the kind words to their parents. "Tell your parents we're thinking of them. They are in our thoughts." The expressions of sympathy are often awkward, sometimes inappropriate, and occasionally offensive. "Be thankful that the Lord called Chris to be by his side." People who acknowledge the death have the best intentions, even when their semantics are poor. Friends may not mention the death and may be afraid to approach the topic, but there are ways to handle these situations.

Chapter 3: The Sibling Oak

This common phase in a sibling's grief is encouraged and rewarded by people who say, "Be strong for your parents" and "They are fortunate that you are such an Oak." I was willing to accept this role and thought that I could protect my parents. I learned the importance of getting past the struggle to remain invincible, the importance of opening myself to grief and dealing with it honestly.

Chapter 4: I'm Not Crazy If I Think I Might Be Crazy

The bereaved experience strong emotions, intense dreams, an attachment to the past, and questionable events. I believed that my brother was with me through the week of his funeral, and that belief tempted me to question myself. I did not know if I could trust myself or if I was manufacturing sounds and feelings to satisfy my need for Chris. I heard about bereaved parents visiting mediums to communicate with their deceased children. My perspective changed with Chris's death because I knew how dominating that need could be. By opening my mind, I learned to accept what I was going through, and to resist judging others.

Chapter 5: The Whys and What Ifs

There are many questions that do not have satisfying answers. If I dwell on the unknowns and the things that I cannot change, then I will just drive myself crazy. I had to learn to accept what I could about the details of Chris's accident, about God's role in his death, and about my current options. Knowing all of the answers would not change the fact that Chris is gone. Regardless of all of the circumstances, I am here now.

Chapter 6: Ignore the Science

The Stages of Grief, the charts and graphs that show the monthly cycles of grief, and the predictability that I read about in grief books taught me nothing. I was disturbed by attempts to categorize emotions and put them in chronological order. Grief is the absence of order, and it is unpredictable. Surviving siblings should forget about the science and accept what they are going through as the reality. I learned to expect and accept my mood swings and strange reactions.

Chapter 7: Salty Smiles

I felt guilty the first time I laughed out loud after my brother died. I felt guilty for forgetting the exact words in our conversations. I also appreciated my sadness and was glad that I felt horrible because I knew that I was supposed to feel sad and horrible. I laughed at myself for crying and sometimes cried while I was remembering a funny moment in our past. Conflicting emotions are a natural part of grief, and guilt comes from many places. Survivors of suicides impose heavy guilt on themselves, and I reason that we only have a small circle of control. I try to work within that circle of control.

Chapter 8: They Ask What It's Like to Live With You

After a few months I felt like everyone else had forgotten about Chris. The world continued to spin, and my friends continued to live their lives as if nothing had happened. My brother's death was old news, and I wondered if anyone remembered. My roommate said that people asked him what it was like to live with me, like I had an affliction. But when I interpreted this question as meaning they were still thinking about Chris and about me, I was comforted by their concern.

Chapter 9: Certain Words

After I lost my brother I found it hard to say that he died. I wanted to say that he lost his life in a car accident; it was taken from him against his will. If it weren't for the accident, he would still be here. Died. Dead. The words are shocking now. They hit too close to home.

Chapter 10: The Dreams We Shared

I lost my future with Chris when he died. We had plans to buy a house together, to make our marks on the world, to be in each other's weddings, to have families of our own, and to share our lives together. When someone dies, that part of your future also dies, and it is difficult to accept.

Chapter 11: The Urge to Glorify

As I accepted the reality of my brother's absence and realized that I would live the rest of my life without him, I developed an intense desire to hold on to him. I wanted to talk about him and tell people how great he was. I wanted to glorify him without turning people away.

Chapter 12: Tell Me a Story

Another common need of surviving siblings is to hear friends and relatives talk about their deceased brother or sister. I want to hear his name so I know that others are thinking about him and missing him. I want to know that I am not the only one who still hurts. Chris's friend John expressed his personal loss in a memorable and touching way.

There are hard days in grief. Hard days may include birthdays, the anniversary of the death date, and many other unpredictable days. My hardest days so far were six months after Chris's accident and the day I lived longer than my older brother. These two days were totally different but both extremely difficult. Such days are inevitable and worrying about them will not stop them.

People are changed by death. The world is a different place, and we are different people. The thought process that I followed to come to terms with my new self has increased my awareness. Relationships within my family have changed. I have an opportunity—I am a new person deciding who I want to be.

Finding a grief counselor and getting involved in a sibling group were important steps in discovering life after loss.

This is the hardest step of all. I've met siblings in my discussion group who had not talked about their deceased sibling for over ten years. Acceptance is vital to surviving positively. When surviving siblings deny the death, they do not give themselves a chance to grieve. When they do not grieve fully, they rob themselves of the opportunity to gain control of their lives again. I gradually came to understand this and live by it.

Afterword: Bridging the Communication Gap

There is a large communication gap between bereaved parents and their living children. Parents don't think their children grieve enough, and children think their parents talk about it too much, making conversations awkward and tense. Some parents won't allow their surviving children to discuss the deceased. Some family members compare grief in a competitive way. Through parent and sibling surveys and in years of discussions with surviving siblings I learned about these situations and thought about ways to bridge the gap.

XIII

INTRODUCTION

The death of a child, no matter how old or under what circumstances, leaves a gaping hole in a family system. Death prompts an examination of relationships, past, present, future, and lost, provoking an emotional response unlike any other.

The death of a sibling has an uncharted impact on the surviving brothers and sisters, who are often overlooked in the details of funerals, burials, and support for parents during the initial and subsequent grieving periods. Yet sibling grief is profound, with universal components that are minimally addressed by grief specialists. Siblings from grade school through adulthood have a shared history with the deceased brother or sister, have developed strong attachments, even while distinct personality styles and conflicts may have emerged, and have expectations of how they will be available for one another in the future. Surviving a Sibling describes this attachment, expectation, and response to loss through Scott Mastley's experience of the death of his brother, Chris.

Death is a shocking end to these expectations, and the grief process prompts an assessment of appreciations, regrets, resentments, wishes, and an awareness of the loss for what could have been, even if the sibling actively tries to suppress this process. A shift in both the surviving siblings' internal world and the external world takes place simultaneously, resulting in a loss of innocence and a redefinition of oneself in the world. **Surviving a Sibling is the first book to examine this process and to offer surviving siblings a voice that may resonate with their own as they grieve this profound loss.**

Circumstances of the death, the family system, and the unique relationship of each sibling to the deceased sibling dictate the differences in the grief process. A catastrophic death allows for no mental or emotional preparation, and the particulars (alone versus with others at the moment of death, accidental versus intentional, natural disaster versus criminal victim, gruesome versus gentle) will contribute to the issues which the surviving sibling reviews, often over and over. The loss of a sibling during war prompts different thoughts, including unanswered information about the circumstances of death (e.g., missing in action, enemy versus friendly fire, political conflict, suffering on the battlefield or at seas). The death of a sibling from illness, particularly prolonged, may prompt not only sorrow but also relief, which may provoke feelings of guilt over one's relief. Finally, the unique relationship of each sibling to the deceased sibling evokes different levels and styles of grief. A sibling close in age, interests, shared history or complementary personality will have a stronger bond and a wash of emotions unlike that of a sibling who may have wished his deceased sibling harm or felt envy of him, and may need to deal with unresolved resentment or guilt.

Scott Mastley's journey through the loss of his brother, Chris, represents an opening for all siblings to risk facing our own grief and reaching out to others for support and recognition. This is a journey that nobody wants to take, and, if we must, we no longer need to walk it alone. Scott is the voice for both Chris and himself, and their sibling relationship was unusually close and open. Such a relationship could only have been fostered in a healthy family system, one that pulled together and grieved openly through their worst catastrophe. Not every reader will have been so fortunate, and to those readers Scott's forthrightness in speaking of his grief may initially seem foreign. But the universality of sibling grief should ring a chord even with those who have buried their grief under anger, depression or silence. <u>Surviving a Sibling</u> will offer ways to meet your needs through your own grief journey; the need for connection with and comfort from the lost sibling, the need for mementos, the need for closeness with friends and family, the need to share memories of the deceased, the need to believe (at least initially) that one must live out one's life for both oneself and the deceased sibling, the need to make it through particularly difficult days, and the need to make sense of the loss. This last need to make sense ultimately requires a redefinition of self that can transform the survivor's experience of life, including identifying and treasuring who and what are important, what it means to use one's time well, and valuing moments in life that others may neglect.

Who should read this book? Obviously, surviving siblings will recognize familiar and possibly thus far unspoken aspects of their grief, and risk reaching out to others to share it. It will appeal not only to those enduring the recent loss of a brother or sister, but also to those of us who have lost a sibling years ago and have elements of unfinished business in the grief and resolution process.

Parents should also be encouraged to learn how their surviving child or children's grief is unique and in need of attention. Similarly, friends of surviving siblings will gain insight into how to offer support and help.

Counselors, clergy, youth ministers and group leaders, physicians and health care personnel, educators, and funeral home staff who come into contact with teens and adults who have lost a sibling not only recently but in the past, should be familiar with the issues identified in <u>Surviving a Sibling</u>. Those of us in these fields may not have experienced the death of a sibling yet, but we all will eventually; and in the meantime we can guide our clients to a voice that resonates with kindred grief.

Scott Mastley presents us with a book short enough to read quickly, thoughtful enough to read a little at a time, and straightforward enough in content to lead us into our own strong responses to grief. <u>Surviving a Sibling</u> fills a void in family grief literature, which has a plethora of books about parental loss, spousal loss, and shifts in family systems without specific extension to sibling reactions. As you read this story of two remarkable young men, take some time to appreciate your deceased sibling(s), and if you are very fortunate, to appreciate your living siblings.

Christiane C. O'Hara, Ph.D.
Licensed Psychologist
August 20, 2000

PREFACE

My brother's death changed my life. It presented my most difficult challenge. I had to learn to live without the one person I thought I could never live without. I had to accept the reality of his death, absorb his absence, and search for smiles. I wanted to grieve fully, but I also wanted to celebrate life in tribute to the positive contributions that my brother, Chris, made to my life.

I wrote <u>Surviving a Sibling</u> for everyone who has experienced or knows someone who has experienced the death of a sibling. It is not a psychologist's description of the stages of grief. It is a personal account of the struggles of surviving a sibling, and in it I answer many of the internal questions that bereaved siblings ask themselves. How do I deal with people who pretend nothing happened? How do I approach friends who are afraid to look me in the eye? Am I going crazy? Why was it he instead of me? How will I survive the rest of my life without him?

Grief is often described as a life-long journey, and like other extended journeys, getting started is usually the hardest part. <u>Surviving a Sibling</u> covers the first few years of my grief process, including counseling and discovering a sibling discussion group in The Compassionate Friends. Real life examples are taken from the conversations I've had with other surviving siblings, from surveys given to bereaved parents and bereaved siblings, and from my personal experience.

Through my experience siblings will learn that they can make it, that they do not have to give up on the rest of their lives. They will also learn how to manage the daily struggles of grief. Jim Dirr, a friend who has buried six siblings and two children, says "You can go around grief, over it or under it. You can even choose to ignore it, but the only way to successfully survive it is to go straight through it."

Death is universal, and everyone is touched by loss at some point in his life. My way of making a positive contribution to the world is writing this book for those who are bereaved, for those who work with and counsel the bereaved, and for those who know and love the bereaved, specifically surviving siblings. Bereaved parents want to know that their remaining children will still live fulfilling lives, and since these younger people may be reluctant to share their thoughts with their parents, <u>Surviving a Sibling</u> traces the thought process of a grieving sibling for them. The book can also help friends by offering examples of what to say and what not to say, by describing the relentless power of grief, and by revealing the often unspoken expectations that we have of our friends.

Over the years I have often heard bereaved parents and siblings express a need for such a book, and those with whom I have shared my manuscript have been deeply moved and have expressed their gratitude. There is indeed a gap in grief literature, and I hope <u>Surviving a Sibling</u> fills it, reaching into the homes and hearts of those who need it most.

SM

Surviving a Sibling

Discovering Life After Loss

XXII

CHAPTER ONE

HEARING THE NEWS

Dad called me at work from his car phone and said with a wavering voice that concerned me, "Chris has been in a car accident. It is serious. I'm on my way to the hospital in Alabama." My stomach dropped, and my heart began to race. I was twenty -five years old, standing in an office building in Atlanta, suddenly reaching for answers.

I asked, " What did they say?"

"They said he was talking when they brought him into the hospital. You need to go home to be with your mother." At this point, I had a look of fear on my face, and my co-worker asked if I was okay. On the phone, Dad's breaths were deep, and as he said, "Scott, please be careful, " I could tell that he was crying. This scared me even more, and a tear rolled down my cheek. We hung up, and I quickly told my concerned co- worker that my brother had been in an accident and that I needed to go home. I wanted to sob because I was so scared and shaky, but I held the bulk of tears in until I was alone in my car.

It was a forty- minute drive to my parents' house, and after about ten minutes, I tried to calm myself. I reasoned with myself. He'll be fine. He's been in car accidents before. You've been through terrible accidents before. He'll have a big scar, and he'll laugh about it and show it to people at parties. Dad said he was talking. Chris, please be okay. God, please let my brother be okay.

Forty minutes seemed like five minutes, and I was home with a dry face and a positive attitude. I planned to comfort my mom and ease her worries. When I walked into the house, she was one step in front of me. She had just walked in and was heading toward the phone to call the hospital. One of my parents' neighbors was there, and Mom seemed to be in control. She was much calmer than I thought she would be, so I assumed that the situation wasn't as bad as I thought. She must have heard something. I can't remember what we said together; it was just nervous chatter. Mom picked up the phone and dialed the hospital in Alabama and told them who she was. She said," How is Chris doing?" Pause. She strained against the phone. She dropped into a kitchen stool and began to scream into the phone, "You can't tell me that! Don't you tell me that!"

I slowly picked up the phone when Mom dropped it and said, "This is Scott Mastley, Chris's brother." The nurse spoke to me. "Scott, I am sorry for telling your mother this way. I have to be honest. I am sorry. I'm so sorry. Scott, Chris didn't make it. He came in; he was talking. He went straight into surgery, but he just didn't make it. I'm sorry, Scott."

I was completely numb. I wasn't crying. My voice was steady. I asked, " Did you hear his last words?" She stalled for a moment and said that his last words were, "I can't breathe." I got her name again, hung up the phone, and walked around the counter to my mother.

She was pleading, thinking out loud, sobbing, and looking up at me with watery eyes. I put my arms around her, and we cried. I was quiet, still in total shock. Mom was saying, " No, no, not my baby. This isn't happening. This isn't happening. This can't be true. How can it be true?" The neighbor comforted us intelligently by staying near and staying quiet. She knew that words would not make a difference. In his book <u>When There Are No Words</u> Charlie Walton says, "At the moment of separation, there really are no words." Time did not exist. The world washed away.

Dad was on his way to the hospital in Alabama, and we didn't want to call him and tell him that Chris was dead; we didn't want him to be alone with the crushing reality of losing his son. We debated. We had no choice; we couldn't let him drive all the way there to choke on his own hope. I called his car phone, and he answered. I said, " Dad, you need to pull over." I heard him quietly moan, " Oh no." I took a deep, shaky breath, and I said, " Dad, Chris didn't make it. They put him under for surgery, and he didn't make it through." Dad groaned painfully; he sobbed into the phone. He asked to speak to Mom. He wanted to be there for her. Mom got on the phone, and together they cried for the loss of their child.

Chris died on December 5, 1994. He was twenty-seven years old. He was a pharmaceutical salesperson and traveled frequently to Alabama to call on doctors. He was close to a hospital in Dothan, Alabama, when he ran a stop sign and was hit by a car that was crossing the intersection. The other car did not have a stop sign and had no way of knowing that Chris was coming through without stopping. There was construction around the intersection, and the view was limited. Chris's car was knocked off the road and into a telephone pole. He was hit on the driver's side and died in the hospital about thirty minutes later from internal injuries.

I just stood next to my mom, completely stunned, and tried to process this enormous, tragic event. I stood for a few seconds with a mind so full of confusion that it felt empty. I was hollow headed from the news. I knew I could stay by my mom and try to comfort her, so that's what I continued to do.

My parents and I don't know why Chris ran the stop sign. We don't know if he didn't see it or if he was tuning the radio or if he realized what he'd done too late. We did not have the chance to talk with him before he died, and information is hard to find. The police gave us a copy of the police report, but it did not tell us much. The man who hit Chris only made contact with us through a letter that his girlfriend wrote to us. I'm guessing that he was afraid we might sue him. It's sad, but I guess that is why he never called us or wrote to us himself. I don't blame him for Chris's death, and I certainly have no plans to take him to court for something he never meant to do. I do wish that he had found the courage and the compassion to write to us or to call us and tell us what happened. We all have unanswered questions.

While Mom and I were churning in our sudden tide of emotions at home, my father had turned around and was driving home alone with the news that he had lost his first born son. I'll never know how horribly alone my dad felt for the few hours that it took him to make it back to Georgia, but every time I think about that trip and how hard it must have been for him, I feel helpless. I can never take that trip away from him. He said he had to pull over a few times because his emotions were threatening his ability to drive. If I think about it, I just ache.

A few hours after we found out about Chris, three of my closest friends and my girlfriend (now my wife) called and asked if they could come out and be with me. I had spent some time in the living room with Mom, and she had people all around her, so I was desperate for some support. I didn't want to make much conversation, but I wanted to have friends near me. I needed to feel their love for me and to know that they were willing to listen if I had something to say. When they arrived, we hugged and cried. I tried to talk, but I couldn't say anything. Since they were old friends, they were also Chris's friends. They were heartbroken by his unexpected death, and maybe they needed me as I needed them. One of them took a week off from work and was with me every day. I didn't ask him to do it; he said it was never a question. I am fortunate to have such great friends.

When Dad pulled into the driveway, I was standing outside with my friends. I went inside and brought Mom outside. The three of us hugged each other for a long time and cried. We didn't know what to say, and I don't remember what was said, but I remember the three of us with our heads together and arms around each other reaffirming the strength of our new family.

As the day progressed, neighbors and friends came by to convey their sympathy and to bring us food. They filled the house with food, and I ate because it was something that I knew I could do. I ate because it was something, anything, to do. I stood in the kitchen, stunned, as sympathetic visitors patted me on the shoulder on their way to the great room, where my parents were sitting. I just stood in the kitchen and answered the door and the phone. I shook hands and directed people to where my parents were sitting. I was in emergency mode. I am usually the person who stays calm and takes control in emergencies. I felt that I was helping by letting people in, pointing them toward my parents, showing them where to put the casserole, answering the phone, and then handing it to Mom or Dad.

The next week was the longest week of my life. My parents asked how I felt about leaving Chris's casket open at the wake. Chris and I had talked about death when he was alive. We both agreed that we would not want open-casket wakes or funerals. We would want people to remember us as we were at our best. Mom and Dad and I decided to view Chris's body before our friends and family arrived at the wake. I didn't want to have to go through it, but I knew my parents needed to see Chris one more time. I was afraid that the scars from his accident would be visible, and I was worried about dealing with them face to face.

People say that viewing the body is important for a sense of closure, that we don't truly believe our tragedy until we see the lifeless form of our loved one. I knew his death was real, and I knew that seeing him would be disturbing, but I did it for my parents.

On the way to the funeral home, we were all nervous. Not one of us knew what it was going to be like to look at Chris's dead body, to know that the life was gone from this body, to know that this would be the last time we would be in the physical presence of his body. My palms were sweating, and my feet were cold.

I tried to get my parents to think as I did about the experience. I told them that we were not going to see Chris; we were going to see the body that he inhabited here—the body he used to get around town. We were going to touch for the last time the hands that he extended for those memorable first impressions. I tried to prepare myself for seeing him by telling myself that I was about to see a lifeless form, a form which was totally familiar to me, a form I had spent my life with, but a form which no longer contained my brother. It was difficult.

I cried immediately at the sight of his body. I touched his hair and his face, and I thought that I would collapse from the sheer weight of his absence, from the desperate yearning I had for his voice, his smile, and his laughter. I tried to say goodbye, but I was unwilling to accept the finality of it all. Saying goodbye to a person whom I was sure I could never live without was a scary thing to do. It's like admitting that you're moving into an entirely new world and leaving everything else behind.

Throughout this process I told myself over and over that Chris was still the same great guy, just spreading his joy in a different place. (The anger had not hit me yet.) I was just trying to deal with the fact that I would never walk next to him again.

It would be much later that I would come across a letter Chris had written to me. It contained one of Chris's poems. One of the lines read, "…a fate conceived to share life as brothers…" The poem was titled "The Gift." Chris was saying that it was silly for us to buy each other birthday presents every year because we were each other's greatest gifts. He wrote about the meaninglessness of material gifts and how we really had no unfulfilled material needs. The gift in the poem was my birth--Chris getting a little brother. We decided not to buy each other birthday gifts any more. Instead we would call or visit and spend time together. We were very close.

I was touched by the words of Richard Harris, the actor and poet, whose sister died. He wrote,
"…And
in her going
the waters of my heart
burst
through the fountains of my eyes
and

day in everlasting night
my mourning kite
will fly
deep in the wilderness of my sight..."

CHAPTER TWO

THE BEST INTENTIONS

I lost my brother, my best friend, and even though I felt the full weight of loss as a surviving sibling, I ended up being a sympathy messenger. I relayed messages of sympathy from relatives, neighbors, and family friends to my parents. They were not sure what to say and usually said something like, "Tell your parents that they are in our prayers." I heard, "Be strong for your parents" and "It must be very hard on them. Tell them that we are thinking of them." I delivered the messages to my parents and secretly wished that someone would recognize my pain.

Concerned friends and family members related to my parents' situation more than to mine. Most of them have children of their own and shuddered when they imagined what their lives would be like without them. They are parents first, friends and neighbors second, so they thought of my parents and tended to overlook my grief. They got caught up reflecting on how horrible it would be to experience the loss of a child, and they just didn't think about me. I was a surviving sibling, but my parents were bereaved parents.

A month after my brother's death, my parents' kitchen table was literally piled with sympathy cards, only one or two of them even mentioning my name. They were addressed to my parents, and even though I was living at home at the time, they were all written to my parents. I remember my mom saying, "Scott, they said they are thinking of us." She sensed that I was feeling left out of everyone's sympathy and tried to include me. I appreciated the thought, but I did feel that I had been forgotten. Friends from our past were writing and calling and saying that they were sorry, but none of them wanted to talk to me about my pain, only about my parents' pain. I have never been a selfish person, but I wanted them to recognize my grief. I believed that it was legitimate. I wanted just one person to say, "It must be really hard for you too. I know how close you and Chris were."

Eventually I ran into some insightful friends who looked me in the eye and asked about me, and stronger bonds were formed there. After two years had passed a few of our mutual friends from college shared their feelings of loss with me. They mentioned their fear of offending or upsetting me and said that they could not imagine how hard it was for me. I was surprised and touched by their words.

Surviving siblings get left out of sympathy often because our friends are not mature enough or experienced enough to know what to say. I knew twelve-year-olds that had never experienced the death of a close friend, and they had enough trouble trying to understand what happened and how the event fit into their lives. I had friends who were twenty years old and were afraid to let down their guards and deal with emotional issues. My friends were in their mid-twenties, and most of them did not want to upset me by bringing up Chris's death, so they just left it alone. Long term family friends who were in their forties and fifties assumed that I knew how they felt for me. Their reactions were similar in that they did not express their concern for me or to me.

It took a few days of phone conversations before I was hurt

by the fact that people apparently didn't think I was grieving the loss of my brother. I'd answer the phone, "Hello?" The reply would be, "Hi Scott. This is ... How are your parents holding up? Who is taking it harder, your mom or your dad? I don't know how they do it. There could be nothing worse. Please tell them they are in our prayers."

I would answer their questions, thank them for calling, and wonder why they didn't say, "Scott, our hearts ache for the three of you."

Sometimes the inappropriate things that people said struck me. "Be thankful that the Lord called him in; he is now serving a higher purpose." No matter what's really happening and no matter what I believe, don't tell me to be thankful when my brother dies. I am not capable of being thankful that my brother is gone, only of being thankful that I shared twenty-five years with him. There is a better way to word that sentiment. Simply saying, "He is in a better place" is much more comforting. I can agree with that.

In a discussion group for surviving siblings I heard stories about people at school or at work who said insensitive things to the bereaved about the lapse of time. "Hasn't it been four months now? You need to move on. It's unhealthy to dwell on it." These words came from people who thought that they were helping. I remember thinking that time passed quickly for them as they went about their lives, and they assumed that I should have also been going about my life, not dwelling on the tragedy. They just did not fully understand how consuming the grief can be.

My good friends and even my girlfriend said some things that hurt my feelings. Most people just do not know what is appropriate and what is not. That is forgivable. On the other hand, if someone was being insensitive in a way that communicated a true lack of caring, I cut that person loose. I didn't need to hang around people who did not care about me, especially then. After I lost my brother, more than ever, I needed people around me who cared about me. And even loving friends and relatives slipped up and did not know it. Since I understood the challenge they faced, wanting to say something but not knowing exactly what to say, I did not hold their comments against them.

When learning of the death of my brother, many people responded by asking, "Do you have any other brothers or sisters?"

I would say, "No. It's just me now."

Then they would always say, "Oh." They wanted to be able to say, "At least you're not an only child." "At least you still have your other sister..." "Appreciate what you've got." They wanted to make me feel better. What they did not know was that even if I had ten living brothers and ten living sisters, I had still lost a life, a life which could never be replaced. I am now an only child, but I don't believe that my grief is worse than the grief of someone with many living siblings. It is simply a bold-faced grief that greets me daily and does not leave my side. I gradually learn to live with it.

How do I deal with people who pretend nothing happened? How do I deal with people who assume that they know how I feel because their pet turtle died when they were little? What do I say to people who start giving me advice or pointing out all of the things that I still have going for me? How do I approach friends who are afraid to look me in the eye?

I'm honest. I'm straightforward. I tell them what makes

me feel better. If they pretend that nothing happened to me, I let them know that I am affected daily by the tragedy. I let them know that it is an approachable subject. If they suddenly keep their distance from me, I put them at ease by sharing my experience. If they are friends worth keeping, then they are friends worth the effort. I call them and say, "I haven't heard from you in a while, and I was hoping that you're not afraid to talk to me because of my brother's death..."

I learned that most people had the best intentions. They were probably thinking about me and wishing me well, whether they let me know it or not. If I thought someone was uncomfortable talking about Chris, I might say, "Since Chris died, you and I haven't talked about him much, and I just want you to know that I don't mind talking about him. I actually enjoy hearing the stories and laughing at them or learning something I didn't know about him." Sometimes I would bring Chris into the conversation just to let people know that I wouldn't freak out at the mention of his name. I wouldn't dwell on him, but I would mention him.

If anyone asked me about Chris or how I was handling his death, I'd take the opportunity to put him at ease first. Other people were nervous about approaching the subject of death. It was scary for them. They didn't know what I was going to do or what I would think of what they said. They were afraid of making it worse by saying something stupid, but they wanted to let me know that they cared. So I said to them, "I think people are worried about bringing Chris up, because they think I might cry. You know, I might cry, but it's not because of what they say. They don't make me cry. If I cry, it's because I miss my brother. I'm touched by what they say. The tears are not always negative. That pain is always there. I appreciate you asking about him, and anytime you want to talk about him, don't be afraid to bring him up."

If people said, "I know how you feel. When my dog died, I was crushed," I was tempted to verbally batter them, but ignorance was the real enemy. So instead of becoming angry at them, I explained what it was like to them. I asked them to indulge me for a few minutes and said, "This is what I'm dealing with. This is how I feel. These are the questions that I wonder about. I just wanted you to know what I'm going through, so you'll understand some of the things I say and do." I even tried asking them how they felt about losing a friend.

I was surprised and comforted by a few of Chris's friends who told me how they were affected. I saw tears in the eyes of normally stoic guys. Two of Chris's male friends said the same thing: "When I found out about Chris, I had to shut my door at work and cry in my office. I couldn't get anything done for a week." A few friends wrote letters to me and told me how much Chris meant to them. If I asked, I learned that I was not the only one missing my brother. I didn't always hear it or see it, but others were thinking about Chris and missing him.

Sometimes a person will call me Chris. I smile because I know that person is thinking about Chris when he's looking at me. I take it as a compliment.

There were insensitive people, co-workers who didn't acknowledge Chris's death or friends who acted as if nothing happened. People said things that made me angry when I thought about them later. It was part of the grief. I reminded myself that most people did not have to go through what I was going through. They had not been where I had been and seen what I had seen. They probably slept well at night; good for them. Fortunately, they won't carry the grief that I carry. I wouldn't wish the death of a sibling on anyone.

One thing I do know is that my friends are my friends for a reason. They care about me, and I care about them. I helped them and helped myself by being open and honest with them. They might have said the wrong things, but they did have the best intentions.

CHAPTER THREE

THE SIBLING OAK

My father says that I am a rock in a crisis. During the weeks following my brother's death, I received much encouragement. When people said, "Be strong for your parents. They need you to be strong for them now," I believed that I could help my parents by taking that advice. I wanted to protect them from any more pain. I wanted to show them that I could not be beaten, and I hoped that they would be inspired by my behavior.

When I was in high school, several of my friends went to a funeral for a boy's father. I was curious about how the boy handled the situation. Did he talk to people? Did he sit limply next to his mother? Did he smile or cry? It was uncharted territory for me, and I wanted to know what a bereaved person did at a funeral. When I asked my friends about it, they said that he had spoken with everyone and thanked them for coming. He had been very strong, having conversations displaying confidence in his future, and everyone was impressed. When I heard that he had been so positive, I thought to myself that if I were ever in his shoes, I would also be strong. When Chris died, this immediately came back to me. I convinced myself that I could do it.

At the wake I walked around and spoke with friends and family, thanking them for coming and thanking them for thinking of us. I shook hands and gave hugs and smiled for concerned women to show them that I was strong. I was a sibling oak and could not be swayed by heavy winds. I was, in my mind, invincible. I remember thinking that nothing in the rest of my life could touch the pain that Chris's death caused, so I had already lived through the worst thing that would ever happen to me. I thought about the old cliché, "Whatever doesn't kill me makes me stronger."

A few months after Chris's accident, a childhood friend of ours died in a car accident, leaving a young husband and a little girl behind. My parents could not make the funeral because it would be too hard for them to be in another funeral. They were not ready to relive the experience. I wanted to go to the funeral to show our deceased friend's surviving brothers that they would be all right. I knew I would cry, and I knew it would be hard, but it was important to me to do what I would normally do. I understood how her brothers felt, and I told them to call me if they ever wanted to talk. I was sad because someone else had to go through what I was going through. I cried for them.

A year later some friends of ours lost their teenage daughter, and my wife and I went to her wake. This time I didn't feel so strong. My stomach hurt from the nervousness of facing an emotional situation. I doubted my ability to hold it together. It was too sad. I saw the young girl's father and wanted to speak with him but I couldn't speak. I opened my mouth to express my sympathy and nothing came but tears. He hugged me, and I cried on his shoulder. That initial feeling of helplessness came back to me when I put myself in his position. Even though I am not a father, I could relate to having a recent and devastating loss. When I look back on that moment, I'm glad that I just cried. It showed the family simply how much I hurt for them.

You should do what you need to do to get through the grief. For me, it meant taking control and being strong and greeting people and saying positive things. That kind of behavior helped me through the first few weeks. But if I had stayed in that mode, I'd be in real trouble today. Sooner or later you have to face your grief and deal with it. Once the wake, the funeral, and the burial were over I needed to face my grief. I had to let it wash over me like a giant wave.

It sent me tumbling through the sediment of my insecurities. I wondered if I would ever be truly happy again. I wanted to go limp and be left alone. At the same time I hoped that friends would call or stop by to talk. I felt a need to reaffirm my love for my parents more than ever before. I think they felt the same way about me, because the three of us expressed our love for each other often, hugged often, and bared our souls more often than we ever had before. I come from a close family and the support and strength that I received from my parents made a great difference. There was no doubt that the three of us would still be a great family, just a different family.

My mother says that her conversations with me now are more like conversations with a peer. I don't know if that is because I am twenty-eight years old or because we survived a terrible tragedy together and can sympathize with each other's feelings. Relationships change, perspectives change, and I still believe that I can protect my parents. Deep down I know that I can't protect them, but part of me still believes it, because sometimes I speak and act as if I do. They don't want to be protected; they probably want to protect me. But we cannot save each other from the grief.

No matter how strong I thought I was I could not protect my parents from the pain. No matter how positive I was, I

could not hide the loss. And no matter how much I thought
I knew of my parents, I could not fully understand the
nature of their grief. Even though we lost the same person,
Chris was who he was in each of our minds.   I lost my
Chris, Mom lost her Chris, and Dad lost his Chris. We each
had our own pain, and pretending to be strong did not take
it away.   The sibling oak worked for a few weeks, but
becoming the grain of sand bounced along the beach within
a giant wave of sadness got me where I am today.
Releasing the emotions renewed my spirits in a painful but
necessary way.

If I held off the pain and didn't set aside time to let it take
me, it would take me anyway in a place and time when I
wish it wouldn't. Now I do what I need to do and always
make sure that I take the time to face my grief.

"You can go around grief, over it or under it. You can even choose to ignore it, but the only way to succesfully survive it is to go straight through it."

- Jim Dirr

CHAPTER FOUR

I'M NOT CRAZY IF I THINK I MIGHT BE CRAZY

My reality is reality. The world I see is the world. The thoughts I have are my thoughts, and the experiences I have are my experiences. Who is to say what is real and what is not? Who is to say what is believable and what is questionable? I know what I see, what I hear, and what I feel. I don't know the boundaries of existence, even if I have my own ideas about them. If no one knows for sure, then who can say what is within the boundaries of existence?

For two weeks after Chris's death I felt his presence. I know it sounds crazy, but I felt him. I did not manufacture it in my mind; I felt him. I could physically feel his arm around my shoulder, and he would say to me, "It's OK. Everything is OK." Sometimes during that period I would feel a sudden immensity, an awareness of Chris's presence. A powerful emotion would hit me, and I would cry. It was realizing that I was involved with more than I ever thought possible. I would leave my friend's house and go outside to talk with Chris. We would have short conversations. He would comfort me and say that he was not going to leave me yet.

During the wake, the funeral, the burial, and several days afterwards I felt like Chris was within me. I felt like him. I caught myself using his mannerisms, saying things that he would say, and listening to music that he liked, music that I normally didn't like. My mouth felt like his mouth, and my arms felt like his arms. I felt very strong and totally prepared for the wake and the funeral and the burial. I told myself that Chris was inside of me, staying with me to help me through the week. I told my girlfriend about it, and she probably thought I was crazy. I wondered if I was creating a comfort zone for myself or if I was really experiencing a connection with Chris.

When I spoke during his funeral to several hundred friends and family members, I was not scared. It was an important thing to do, and I was grateful for the opportunity. I felt that Chris was with me as I spoke. I believed that he heard my words, and I was encouraged. I appreciated the opportunity to make his funeral personal, to distinguish it.

After the ceremonies and after the people and food were gone, there was quiet. It was time to lift up my face and look the new world in the eye. I still felt strong and confident about the future. Then one day, about two weeks after Chris's death, I felt him leave. I had a dream the night before that I was with a group of friends, and we were driving to a bar. Chris was with us, but he was sitting in the back of the car. I was in the front. I saw him in the back, and he acknowledged my surprise with a calm nod of his head and a sympathetic smile. When we reached the bar and began to file inside, Chris did not go inside. Our friends all went inside the bar, but Chris and I stayed outside to have a talk. He said that he was going soon and that he was OK. He said that things were different but nice. I asked him questions, and he answered them. When I woke up, I was sad but comforted. He told me goodbye.

That day I felt him leave. I physically felt his presence leave. My body felt totally different than in the past two weeks. I felt cold and alone and vulnerable. I felt like me.

I thanked Chris for being so selfless, for staying with me, for being a wonderful earthly brother and an enlightening supernatural presence. I believed in that connection, even though I knew that the physical sensation was gone. I knew that Chris had moved on, but I did not doubt that he had been with me. I still do not doubt it.

I questioned the feelings and the conversations after they happened but never while they were taking place. I wondered if I could trust myself, especially after going through such an enormous life-changing event. I tried to be rational, but the reality of Chris's presence was undeniable. I told myself, "You're not crazy if you think you might be crazy." It's when you stop questioning that you might actually be crazy. Even after three years I believe whole-heartedly that Chris was caring and generous enough to delay his heaven to help his little brother through a rough time. He was that kind of guy.

Dealing with Chris's death changed my perspective on something else. I used to think that anyone who went to seek the assistance of an intermediary was foolish. Now, after struggling with the desire to hear from Chris again, to get a sign from him or to communicate with him in some way, I understand the urge to believe in a connection. The need to know that my brother still knows I'm thinking about him is strong.

I have never sought the services of anyone who claimed to be able to speak with the deceased. I have never been to a psychic, but I have a broader view of the concept. There are things in the world which are beyond us, things that we do not understand. How can we judge what we do not understand? You can go to a medium, and learn something that you've wanted to know. Maybe you'll learn that you don't believe a word of it, but maybe you'll learn that your sibling is proud of you and knows what you are doing with your life. Some people say it is a waste of time and money to visit a psychic, and the television commercials have not done much to help the case. Some people say that the experience opened doors for them. I say do what helps. I believe in options, and that is certainly one.

I had conflicting emotions, questionable experiences, dreams that seemed real, and I used to wonder if I was the only one. At a meeting for bereaved people I listened to bereaved parents and siblings describe the after-death communications that they had shared with their deceased loved ones. One woman described an important event involving her husband, his deceased father, and their two -year old child. Her husband was watching television when his deceased father suddenly spoke to him. He recognized the voice immediately and did what he was told to do. He got up and went to look in the pool in the backyard. He was horrified to see his two- year old son under the water. He pulled his son out of the water and called an ambulance. Their son was saved. I've heard things that I never would have believed before Chris's death. Now I am not so quick to judge.

"At the same time that we feel more profoundly and gratefully connected to friends and family, we have a sense that all of us dwell in mystery, that we are connected to earth and sky, to the rhythms of the universe, to the whole range of living things in ways we do not understand."

- Martha Whitmore Mickman

CHAPTER FIVE

THE WHYS AND WHAT IFS

When Chris died, I was twenty-five years old. I felt that I had my entire life ahead of me, and I was looking forward to sharing it with my brother. We were very close. When I understood that Chris was dead, my world slowed quickly to a grinding halt, and I continued to hold on with all I had. I once heard someone say, "You're OK if you can hold on to a blade of grass and not fall off the edge of the world." It has been over three years since the accident, and many times I felt as if my link to the world was about as weak as a blade of grass. I held on to that blade and was thankful for it.

After Chris's death I fought to accept a simple philosophy. I fought self-doubt, disillusionment, anger, depression, and isolation. I fought to live this idea: I can choose to sink into the murky waters of whys and what-ifs and stagnate on the bottom or I can choose to learn from Chris's life and celebrate my life by surviving as successful survivors do—finding reasons to go on, recognizing moments of connection, working for some peace and eventually some happiness.

A definition of surviving is "rising to act." Rising to act is necessary. After Chris died, I wanted to sink. I knew that if I did not rise to act, to take control of my life again, I could keep sinking. To reach what was an acceptable level of progress for me, I had to rise. I made myself rise.

I can't help thinking about my deceased sibling, but I can determine the kinds of thoughts I have. The human brain is powerful, and I handle the controls. I have the ability to choose, so I choose healthy thoughts. If I catch myself focusing on the whys and what ifs, I gather myself and decide to focus on thoughts that won't drag me down. I think of positive memories that make me laugh. I think of stories that I always enjoyed telling about my brother. I think detailed thoughts, remembering every little thing about defining moments in our relationship.

I can always think of the time that Chris left for college. We spent a lot of time together before he left, and we realized in that time how much we cared for each other. We became very close, but we were still at that stage where we did not express our mutual love and respect for each other. Chris was two years older than I was, and I was still in high school. I was excited for Chris, but I did not really want him to leave. The morning after he left for college in Nashville, I found a letter under my pillow from Chris. It said that he was proud of me and that he hoped I would call and write to him at school. He said he loved me and would miss me. It was a defining moment in our relationship. From that point on, we weren't afraid to say, "I love you," even if we did add, "man" to the end of the statement. I read it a hundred times during the next few weeks, and I cried every time.

Crying doesn't always mean that I am depressed; it just means that I am expressing the power of life. I'm feeling my sibling's effect on my life and realizing how it helped to shape the person I've become.

There is a Lyle Lovett song entitled "Simple Song" that my brother and I enjoyed. His favorite line was "...Hear my words with faith and passion…" He just liked faith and passion. I like to think that Chris worked well with faith and passion. He always brightened up a party, charmed pretty girls, cheered up his little brother, and made his parents proud. My favorite line from the same song is "…And when you find the one you might become, remember part of me is you."

I believe in simple truths and consequences for actions. I ask why. Why was Chris taken from us? Why did it have to be him? Why did this happen? Why didn't the other driver see Chris? Why did Chris run the stop sign?

Some people would ask why God would do such a thing. I can only ask that if I believe that God does such things. I've tossed the questions around and looked at them from every angle and still cannot come up with an explanation that totally satisfies me. The challenge is to find an explanation that I can live with.

I don't want to believe that God hand- picks people to be hit by cars, to drown, to die of carbon monoxide poisoning. I believe in accountability, so I can't say that Chris's accident was someone else's fault. I wish I could say that. I want to say it. I wish I could pin the blame on someone, but I doubt that it would make me feel better.

I've seen too many surviving siblings suffer through maddening court cases. Two sisters lost their brother in a vehicle accident that was caused by a driver who was drunk and on drugs. The guy had several DUIs and still had a valid driver's license. They knew who killed their brother. They did not benefit by knowing who was at fault. They found a target for their anger and tried to do the community a service by getting the offender off of the road. When that didn't happen, they saw the ineffectiveness of our court system and were even more frustrated. The guy was convicted after a few years waiting for trial, but the judge forgot to swear in the jury, so he was freed. It only served to make them more miserable. It was emotionally draining and extremely frustrating for them. They got no justice, and they were forced to revisit the images of the accident again and again. Knowing who is responsible does not change a thing. The pain continues, because it comes from the death of our sibling.

The only explanation I can live with is that Chris ran a stop sign and was hit by another car. I don't believe that it was part of a grand design. He was not fated to be in that spot at that time, eventfully travelling for twenty-seven years to get there, but he was there. He chose to take that route and accidentally ran a stop sign. I wish he hadn't.

What if he had taken another route? What if he had not gone to work that day? What if he had taken another job, one that did not require travelling? What if…? The whys and what ifs are endless. I could drive myself crazy asking these questions. On the other hand, the point of view that the circumstances of the death don't matter, that it is only the reality of my sibling's absence that matters, won't do the trick either. I will always remember as much as I know of how, when, and where it happened.

It is natural to wonder. I wish I knew exactly what happened and why it happened. I have a difficult time with the fact that I don't know if Chris can see me, because I cannot see him. I don't know for sure where he is. Does he know where I am and what I am doing? I was told that it's important to live the life I wanted to live, not the life that Chris wanted to live. In many ways we wanted the same things, and I still want to make him proud. Maybe if I'm proud of myself, of where I am and what I'm doing, then

I'll know that Chris would also be proud of me.

It's OK to wonder, but it is unhealthy to burden myself with questions that have no ultimate answers. It is up to me to decide what I believe and to accept the answers that I can live with. Some people turn to religion for their answers, some don't. I believe that death is not the end of existence; it's just the end of that body. I've learned not to torture myself by asking why and what if too often. I search myself and find what I can accept, realizing that there may be no definite answers to some of my questions. I choose to survive, to do what I need to do to find the force of my life again.

CHAPTER SIX

IGNORE THE SCIENCE

I claim to know nothing about the science of grief. I am not a psychologist. I don't know the chronological stages of grief or the biological explanations for the way my body feels. A graph of emotions will not change the way I feel. I do know that emotions are exhausting, and if any science could describe the order of emotions after a loss, it would be the science of chaos, the absence of order.

I might think of a specific memory, begin to cry, then laugh out loud as I remember something else. I might have a normal week and then be blindsided by grief for one day. I might not cry at all for a month or I might wonder how my body can still produce tears after all I've cried. I might be confused because, as I remember the brother I loved, I have two conflicting emotions; I love thinking of Chris and the wonderful times we had together, but I can't stand the reality of the loss. Even when I have positive memories, the memories remind me that I would prefer to have my brother than to have memories. Over time, the positive memories have become comforting. The loss doesn't go away, but it doesn't knock me to my knees every time I acknowledge it.

I ignore the science. I've seen charts of emotions, graphs of guilty feelings, time lines for grief, and I've read explanations that were supposed to explain something about the way I felt. They did nothing for me. If there were really a pattern that all bereaved siblings followed in their grief, I would know exactly what to say to other surviving siblings. I would know where they are in their grief. I could tell them how they were going to feel at three months, six months, and on the one- year anniversary of their sibling's death date. People who have not experienced such a loss say things like, "It's been four months. It's time to get yourself together and move on..." Other people don't fully understand how I am affected by my grief. Their time frames are not my time frames.

I hear about the "Stages of Grief." According to my experience, the stages of grief are mumbo jumbo. The beginning of grief is not forwardly logical. With hindsight I can break down my past emotions and experiences into a logical sequence. I can see where one thing caused something else, but there is no clear reason why some days hit me and some days don't. There may be triggers in my sensory perception like songs, sights or smells that remind me of my brother. I might just be sitting in my room and start crying. There doesn't need to be an explanation for that. It just is what it is. There are all emotions all the time and some emotions are closer to the surface than others. There are moments of numbness. There are dreaded days and days that will surprise me with a hint of joy. It is difficult to predict.

The closest I can come to assigning an order to the grief process is to say that it is suffocation at first, then grief with gasps of life, and then life with grief. I will always deal with grief, some days more effectively than other days. I can learn to accept the grief and once again live a full life. Like other surviving siblings I am put to the test, but I can make it. I can survive successfully because I have managed to do it. I am here now.

If I learned one thing from my brother's death, it is that there are only basic truths, and everyone knows them. I don't have to tell you what they are because you feel them in moments of glory, moments of sadness; you feel them when you cry in a movie. When you think you might be in love, when your best friend makes you proud, you feel the foundation of happiness. Defining bereavement is taking too much information, too many memories, and too much confusion and putting it all into a bottle that can only hold a hundred tears.

Random moments that were once insignificant return to me and overload my senses. I see Chris in so many ways. When I drive I replay the things he said and the things he did, and I cry. The tears may come from different places. I cry angry tears, desperate tears, and I also cry thankful, almost joyful tears. If I think about the question of fairness and try to figure out why it happened to my family, I exhaust myself with grief. If I remember Chris's flaws and the reasons we loved him so much, I laugh through my tears. Sometimes it hurts to cry so intensely, but other times it lifts a great weight from me. After three years, I can see all of this clearly, but the first few weeks weren't so clear.

The week after Chris's accident was the slowest week of my life. My grief began on a Monday when I heard the news. We had the wake on Wednesday, the funeral on Thursday, and the burial on Saturday. A full week of events took place before I could face my grief. I just told myself over and over, "I just need to make it to Tuesday, to Wednesday, to Saturday." I felt a dull ache, the combination of sadness and numbness. I longed for Chris's presence. I remember thinking, "I'll ache eternally for his smile."

The pain went nowhere during the first week. It was heavy

and hanging all over me, dragging me down, making me clumsy. I was too sad to fall asleep. It was just too much to try to process. My mind took oceans of emotions and funneled them through the corners of my eyes. I lay in bed asking, " Why did this happen? How did it happen? Who was involved in the accident? Why was our future stolen? How could someone who was so full of life lose that life?"

I found no answers to my questions. I struggled just to understand the reality that I was never going to see Chris again. I thought of him constantly and tried to replay conversations and events to make sure that I wouldn't forget them. Over time, there were days when I could catch myself forgetting about the pain for twenty seconds. I could laugh at my parents' dog chasing a frog in the driveway. Maybe I wasn't forgetting about it. Maybe I was learning to carry it with me. I didn't know.

Learning the Stages of Grief did not clarify the reasons behind my emotions, did not help me to predict my future feelings, and did not satisfy any need that I had to understand what I was going through. In writing this book three years after my brother died I am still trying to figure it all out. I know that it is possible to survive and to live well again. I know that there are days that flatten me, and I know that I had to work to develop a positive approach to my new life. The hurt is there, and the empty feeling is still there sometimes, but not all the time. We are all individuals. I choose to leave the science to the experts and focus on what I need to do to get by.

CHAPTER SEVEN

SALTY SMILES

During my first few months of grief, I worried about forgetting Chris's voice or his laugh. I recounted memories of our lives together over and over as if I were reviewing information for a test. I wanted to make sure that important moments would not be lost. I wrote down phrases that Chris used, described mannerisms that he employed, and I wrote about some of those important moments. I did everything I could to retain all of Chris in my mind as vividly as possible. I searched for video footage and any audio recordings of his voice.

The fear of forgetting is common. I know that I could never forget my brother, but I don't have quite the grasp on all of my memories that I wish I had. I catch myself filling in gaps of remembered conversations with my own words. Sometimes it's a struggle to remember who was there, where we were, what actually happened, and what came out of it. It may be the grief. The mind-numbing experience results in the dulling of things like thinking clearly and remembering. It may be that I try to remember everything at once, and it's just too much. It's real. Most surviving siblings have experienced this stress.

It's like swimming in Jello. I can try as hard as I want, but I am still in Jello. I do enough to stay afloat, slurp a little Jello if it's my flavor, and hold out until I'm back in the water where those strokes will count. Time will help to ease my mind, and I will feel alive again. The memories will be there for me because they're important to me. There is no better memory aid than an important moment.

I had some awkward moments of laughter in the first few months. I needed them, and I took advantage of them. They eased my mind and gave my heart a breather. I had salty smiles. I laughed at myself for crying, laughed because I couldn't believe how much I was crying. I watered up while smiling about positive memories. I cried during a commercial and laughed at myself for being such a sucker.

At first there was a bit of guilt associated with happiness. Why would that be? Why would I feel guilty about feeling happy? Sometimes I thought I should feel terrible every second of the day. If I did not feel bad, then I didn't feel bad enough. I brought up sad thoughts to make myself feel sad again. Well, I felt bad enough without having to try to feel bad, so I decided to accept the happy moments when they came. I tried to search for them in friends and family, to recognize them, and appreciate them.

If you wrestle with yourself over feeling guilty and you deny those fleeting moments of positive remembrance, you will end up on your back. Instead of struggling against your naturally occurring thoughts and emotions, think of yourself as the referee in the wrestling match. You are the one who steps in and controls the action. Don't let one competitor (guilt) dominate unfairly.

I have spoken with many survivors of siblings who committed suicide, and in my experience, they feel especially guilty. They might feel responsible. They wonder what they could have done to prevent the suicide. They wonder if they did not share enough of their love. They may go over and over unanswered questions. I can understand where the guilt would come from, and I can understand how they might examine the role they played in their sibling's life. But it brings me back to the same point—we can never reclaim our lives if we focus too much on the past. Regardless of what happened, we are here now trying to get by.

My brother did not commit suicide, so I cannot say that I know what it is like. I always wish that I had done more, but in reality I probably did wonderfully. The suicides probably have nothing to do with the actions of siblings. People who unsuccessfully attempted suicide say that when a person commits suicide, he has created an optionless world in his mind. The people around him cannot change that.

A friend of mine from the Compassionate Friends Sibling Group talked about a friend of his who tried to take his own life. His friend survived the attempt and said that he was beyond reason when he tried to kill himself. He said that he was so far down that no one could have convinced him to look around and feel the love of his friends or family. He had created a world in his mind in which there were no options, and he felt as if he had no free will to resist the urge.

Assigning guilt to myself will not help my sibling, and it will not help me. I think of the considerate things that I used to do. I think of the way Chris felt about me. I think of the love that we shared and realize that it was not my fault. I am here now, and I must make a choice. Will I let the guilt consume me or will I address my future? It is very difficult to imagine, but the future holds some happiness. I tell myself not to rush it, but to give it a chance.

CHAPTER EIGHT

THEY ASK WHAT IT'S LIKE TO LIVE WITH YOU

After Chris's death I shared an apartment with a friend. On Chris's birthday my roommate asked me how I was doing. I said that the day was tolerable, that I was doing OK. He said that he didn't want to remind me of it by bringing it up. I told him I was thankful that he had asked about my day. I needed a friend to care. No one besides my parents was talking to me about Chris. When I asked my roommate if our friends ever said anything about Chris's death or about my family, he said, "They ask what it's like to live with you."

I guess that they were curious, as I was about the boy's father who had died while I was in high school. They were also cautious. At first I was upset that my friends wouldn't talk to me openly about my grief or about Chris. I was angry with them for not recognizing something that had devoured my life. I was surprised that they had asked my roommate about living with me. He had responded that there are times when I am quiet but that I don't bring him down or act more strangely than normal.

After calming down, I was glad to know that other people were thinking of Chris and thinking of my grief, even if they weren't talking to me about it. At least I knew that I was not alone in missing him. I think they were afraid of opening a wound, and that is why they did not approach me. What they did not realize is that the wound is wide open every day. I learn to live with it.

Chris's absence is as present as the air I breathe. I think about him and the life we shared every day. I think about the example he set for me and the standards he set for himself. I think about his love for his family. There is no reminding, no re-opening. There is acknowledgement of grief and loss and feeling. In asking a simple question, "How is your day going?" friends can recognize the feelings as being present. It is a wonderful feeling to have a friend who cares enough to overcome the common fear of expression to show concern.

Some people are afraid that if I cry in response to something they said that they made me sad. They think they caused my tears. Even though I should have known better, I felt this way about my mother. I thought that she was fragile, and I would choose my words carefully because I did not want to make her cry. It has taken me a long time to realize that the crying is not a direct response to things people say.

The crying is a symptom, a visual cue, sometimes uncontrollable, that there are strong feelings present, feelings that are not staying inside any longer. Those strong feelings may be connected to a joyful memory, a funny story, or a little fear associated with the fact that we are now living in a new world. This world makes no apologies. When I cry in a conversation, it is because of the same reasons that I cry in a movie or while reading a novel; it is cathartic. I am simply letting myself FEEL.

This is a huge step for me and one that has made all of the difference. It is pivotal. Before Chris died, I rarely cried. I knew men who could cry, and I believed in the therapeutic value of crying, but I couldn't make it happen. Even if I needed to cry and wanted to cry, even if I locked myself in my room and mooned over every reason I had for crying, I didn't cry. The only time I misted up was in movies, when I was caught up in the lives of characters. I used to go to certain movies for that reason alone. I needed to cry, and welling up a little was as close as I could get.

With Chris gone, I have shed worlds of tears. At first I cried because I wanted my brother back, because it wasn't fair, because I felt cheated, because I couldn't imagine continuing to live my life without him. But now the reason I cry is not because I am sad or happy. It may sound naïve, but I cry simply because I am feeling life, feeling the true moments in life which define us, recognizing the past and the future and letting it all flow over me, recognizing the existence of more than I know.

Several friends pulled me aside about a year after Chris's death. They apologized for avoiding the topic and acting like nothing had happened. They mentioned their cautiousness about dealing with something new and something so sensitive. They said they wanted to talk about it but didn't know what to say. They wondered what it was like for me.

This is what it's like to live with me. I am thinking of all these things. I am pinpointing memories and calling them up. I am feeling sad about what was and could have been. I am crying when I am alone and sometimes asking for more time to be alone. I am doing strange things like wearing an old shirt with holes in it because it belonged to Chris. I am keeping many of the feelings to myself, even though I know I should air them. I think I am sparing the people who love me by not burdening them with my grief. I know better, but sometimes I still want to be self-contained. I am learning to live with the grief daily, and I am finding more moments of happiness as time passes.

The world is full of individuals pattering through their lives in meaningful ways and trying to leave something behind. I am affected by my loss, but it does not finish me. I may be detained or detoured, but I will continue to move and progress in some fashion. I will achieve life.

CHAPTER NINE

CERTAIN WORDS

My mother paged me while I was at work this afternoon, and I called her at home. She asked if I would like to go see a movie. Her question triggered many thought waves. I wanted to go with her, to be with her, but I couldn't just leave work. I wish I could have protected her from the loneliness. She was having a rough day like me, and I needed to talk. How was dad at work? Was he struggling to perform like me? Did he have to concentrate to finish anything?

I regret not doing what is most important. I should have talked with my boss and left work to be with my mother when she wanted to spend time with me. I feel great sympathy for my parents, but I have to admit that I don't grieve with them. We don't grieve together. We talk about it, but we usually grieve on our own. I'm guilty of trying to protect them in the same way that my friends try to protect me.

My parents say, "We are here for you. Call us when you need us."
I say, " I know. I will."
They say, "You haven't. You know we think about it every day, all the time. We can talk about it."
I say, "I don't want to be depressing."
They say, "You can be depressing with us. It is depressing."
I say, "I know. I know. I'm here for you too. I just don't want to come out there and cry. I want to be positive."

I think about how I always say "it" referring to the car accident, to Chris's death. I should say "him." I say "it" because the accident took his life; it was the turning point. I am really talking about Chris, his life, and his absence. I'm tired of thinking about the accident, picturing the scene, remembering Chris's last words, and imagining him as he arrived at the hospital. These things are too painful.

It is hard to say that Chris died or that he is dead. If I say that he died, in my mind, it implies that he was sick or weak and that he could not sustain himself any longer. He was vibrant and healthy and full of life. The life didn't leave him on its own; it was knocked out of him in a car accident.

I know that there are people who are walking along the street when they suddenly die. They were also vibrant and full of life. This is just an example of one of our little struggles. I hear surviving siblings say, "My brother was killed in a car accident. A tumor killed my sister. My little brother lost his life to an accidental drug overdose. My big sister didn't make it through surgery." We generally prefer to say that something is responsible for taking the life of our sibling. Saying that he died on a Monday doesn't place accountability for his death on any event. If the event had not occurred, our siblings would still be here, so we feel a need to mention the event in connection with the death.

It is difficult to say that my brother is dead. It is shocking to hear myself say it. The word is final and leaves no questions. It lets you know that Chris is gone forever. He's not going to show up later in the evening. He is not going to call. He is not going to write a letter. He is dead. I hate to say it. He did die and he is dead, but I squirm when I say it like that. It is so matter of fact.

"When a person is born, we rejoice, and when they're married we jubilate, but when they die we try to pretend nothing happened."

- *Margaret Mead*

CHAPTER TEN

THE DREAMS WE SHARED

Chris and I had big plans. The year before he died we spent several weekends driving through Atlanta neighborhoods looking for an affordable house. Chris was going to buy the house, and I was going to rent a room from him. He called me excitedly one night and talked about his girlfriend and the things they had said to each other. He said that she was the one. He had worked hard, landed his dream job in Atlanta, found his ideal mate, and was ready to settle down and carve out the second phase of his life. My only concern was that they continue to date for a long time so I could still rent a room from him.

We set goals and deadlines for future achievements. We made lists of things we'd like to do. We lived about fifteen minutes away from each other, and we talked on the phone a few times a week. I was excited for Chris. I was looking forward to sharing a house with him.

I was sure that Chris would get married and have children before I would, but his death changed everything. When I bought my first house I hoped that Chris approved. I thanked him as I walked through the house for always supporting me, for helping my parents teach me how to be responsible, for setting a great example. I was proud of the house partly because I knew that Chris was proud of me for getting it.

We used to talk about our weddings. He would be my best man and I would be his best man. When I got married, the kindest and most loving man in the world, my father, was my best man. In the weeks leading up to the wedding, I worried about how I would feel standing up in front of the crowd without Chris. I visualized the wedding and what we would look like standing up there. I imagined Chris and Dad standing next to me, and then I pictured the scene without Chris. I wondered if my longing for Chris would interfere with the joy that I should be feeling. I wondered if people would be saying to their dates, "His brother died in a car accident a few years ago. They were real close." Getting married without my brother was tough, but my parents were there, my friends were there, and luckily, my fiancée was there too.

It was the kind of moment that took me over. I knew that Chris wasn't there, but I also knew that I was on the verge of formalizing a wonderful bond. Doreen asked if I was okay when we were at the altar, and I was. I really was. I was happy to be getting married to an amazing woman, and I felt that Chris was watching us. I knew that he would have been there if he could have been there. Maybe he was there. Maybe there is more to life than I can see. I don't know. I was just glad to witness my life progressing.

Marriage was a major milestone, and fatherhood will be another one. It breaks my heart that my children won't know my brother. I can show them photos and tell funny stories, but my story telling ability is only so good. I won't ever be able to truly and fully present my brother to them. I would be a different person if I had not grown up with him, and I wish my children could know that part of me. I don't have any children yet, but I think about them when I see our friends' babies.

People ask about our plans for children. We plan to have two children for many reasons, and one of them is that we don't want to take the risk of losing one child and being childless. It is a little fatalistic and a horrible thought, but I have met many bereaved parents who are grieving over the loss of their only child. These are things that most people don't think about.

The dreams that Chris and I shared were lifelong dreams going as far as how old we would be when we made our first millions. We wondered who would get married first and what we would name our children. We talked about the kind of people we wanted to be as adults, and we promised to learn from the love and sacrifice of our parents. Making millions may be a challenge, but I will certainly live out the rest of my dreams. I will live them for myself and for the satisfaction of telling Chris what it was like one day.

Chris's life wasn't long enough to deliver all of his dreams, but if he had the same basic dreams as the rest of us—to be fully loved, respected, and admired—he lived them completely. I've heard many surviving siblings say, "My brother packed more living into fifteen years than most people do in a lifetime." I can learn from that. How much am I living? How often am I on the edge of realizing a dream? How persistent are my efforts to attain my goals? I think of the things that I once took for granted and take lessons from regrets.

This issue is limitless. Chris isn't here to slap me on the back or give me a high-five, but I know that he would if he were here. That knowledge has to suffice. His love for me is comforting still. The memories of making plans with him are comforting. Hearing his voice in my head is comforting. I am going to live my life to its fullest potential, and I suggest that everyone else do the same. I've come to believe that the purpose of life is not to amass the most toys or to make the most money but to be the best you can possibly be. I don't want to leave any part of my potential untapped. I strive to be irrepressible. This world can't beat me. Chris is on my side.

CHAPTER ELEVEN

THE URGE TO GLORIFY

Chris was always athletic. He played baseball, basketball, and tennis as a child. He played soccer in his teens and set records on the high school swim team. He was six feet tall and in college at Vanderbilt bulked up to two hundred pounds—most of the extra weight in his face and belly. We called him Maynard because of the physical resemblance to Maynard Jackson, Atlanta's Mayor. His other nicknames included Leadbelly, The Reverend, and Gramps. He took them all in stride and even wanted a T-shirt with Maynard Jackson's picture on it. At Vanderbilt he would chuckle and say, "The fatter I get, the more women love it. They think it's cute."

There was something about him that the women loved, but when he moved back to Atlanta he lost forty pounds running and dieting. He was back to fighting weight, and he had set his sights on settling a sibling rivalry.

When Chris and I saw each other we arm-wrestled. It had become a tradition. We always talked it up before hand and told each other how badly he would be beaten. We flexed. We bragged about how much we'd been working out. It was all just fun, but Chris had not beaten me in a few years. As he was getting into shape and feeling stronger, he warned me that the day was near—the day when he would end my reign. He would challenge me in front of two witnesses, Mom and Dad, and he was planning to knock my knuckles through the table.

There was much as stake. He was my older brother. I had beaten him so many times that he felt the need to assert himself and remind me who's boss. In Chris's words, and he would say this constantly while we were arm-wrestling in an attempt to make me laugh, "Who's your daddy?" When the big day came Chris had the will to win, and all I had was overconfidence. He took me down in the presence of those who gave me life, and there was no shame. He beat me, and I knew I wouldn't hear the end of it, but I didn't care. It was a funny thing, two men bragging and arm wrestling in front of their parents. I didn't get the chance to challenge him again.

I am full of stories that I'd like to share. The urge to glorify my brother is strong. I want to fill you with my stories of Chris, show you pictures of him and give you the history of each one. I want to present him so thoroughly to you that you know him, appreciate him, and love him as I do. I want to carry on his legacy.

This is an urge that most surviving siblings have in common. I want to tell other people about my sibling. I want them to know how great Chris was. I wonder if I am the only one who remembers the funny things that he did, the intelligent things that he said, and the respectable life that he lived. I want to make sure that my brother is not forgotten.

I think a balance is important. Sometimes I resist the urge to keep talking about Chris and tell myself that I might overdo it. Sometimes I ask a friend to indulge me and listen to a story I want to tell. Sometimes I just listen and think about Chris. He had flaws like the rest of us, but I remember them with a grin. My memory of him is so positive and so powerful that I want to share it with everyone. I have to concentrate to remember his annoying habits.

Why would someone want to remember the annoying habits of their deceased sibling? Every part of him was part of him. Without his minor imperfections he would have been someone else. Humans have flaws. What sets us apart is the way in which we deal with our own imperfections. Chris was not an angel, and he wasn't perfect. He was smart, funny, always upbeat, ambitious and organized, and he was loving. He'd walk across a room just to give me a hug, and I remember that too. I remember all of him that I loved, and that is all of him.

CHAPTER TWELVE

TELL ME A STORY

The other day a friend reminded me of something my brother used to say. If Chris could not explain how something happened, he would simply say that it was magic. This probably does not mean much to you, but it means a lot to me. I can picture him saying it and people laughing around him. I don't know why that little bit of information slipped my mind, but it did, and I was glad to get it back. My friend had given me a little piece of my brother.

What about hearing these stories helps me? On the surface the stories let me know that I am not alone in my grief. When friends share their tales with me, I can see how my brother touched their lives. I can feel that Chris is missed. It's important for me to know that my brother is not forgotten. It may appear as though everyone is moving on with life and not looking back, but I've found that they cannot forget a friend who touches their lives.

After Chris's funeral our friends gathered at the house where Chris had been living to share some stories, drink some beers, and celebrate the life of my brother. There were many tender moments that night as we traded our favorite of Chris's sayings or the funniest things that he did, but nothing touched me more than a tribute that was made without words.

John lived in our neighborhood growing up, and he and Chris were best friends, lifelong friends. They both loved to play their guitars and listen to the Rolling Stones. John was talented and dedicated to his talent, playing the guitar. Chris was less talented, but he was determined to learn to play well. Their paths split after high school while John was putting in endless hours of practice and Chris was out pursuing dreams that held more promise for him than music. He knew that he did not have the natural ability that John did, but he always loved the idea of being a guitar player. He loved the fact that John was making a living playing his guitar.

When Chris was twenty-seven, he moved to Atlanta and began a new job. He bought a new electric guitar with his signing bonus, one with a maple neck, one he had wanted for years. He called John to tell him about it.

After Chris died, I thought about his things and what we should do with them. When I thought about his new guitar and his amplifier, I thought of John. I knew that Chris would want John to have his guitar, because no one would appreciate it and use it as much as John would. No one would know what it meant to Chris as John would. I called John and told him that we wanted him to have the guitar, and he was touched. I told him to get it after the funeral.

John, his wife and their new baby daughter were at our gathering after Chris's funeral. After an hour or two had passed, I wondered if they were still at the house. I hadn't seen them in a while. I walked upstairs to the room that Chris had been staying in to see if John remembered to take the guitar with him when he left. As I got to the top of the stairs, I heard the sound of music coming from Chris's room. I tapped gently on the door and stepped into the room.

John's wife and daughter were silently lying next to each

other on the bed. As I walked in, they sat up on one elbow and smiled sympathetically at me. John was sunken into Chris's chair next to the bed. His eyes were closed. He held Chris's maple necked guitar in his lap, and he was quietly playing the blues. His head was tilted back, and tears were squeezing out of the corners of his eyes and sliding heavily down the contours of his face. John worked his fingers along the neck of the guitar, and he made it sing about how he was feeling. The chords ran deeply through me.

He wasn't doing it for me; he was doing it because there was no better way to show and share his emotion with his family and with Chris. He was in Chris's room on Chris's guitar; he was playing with him one last time, and he was expressing his pain.

In simple words, it was a grand tribute. It was one of the most touching moments of my life, and I will never forget the feeling that I got from John making that guitar wail so quietly and sweetly. My presence in the room only lasted a few minutes, but the meaningful impression from those few minutes will stay with me for the rest of my life.

CHAPTER THIRTEEN

SIX MONTHS AND TWELVE DAYS

The six-month anniversary of Chris's death was one of my toughest days. I was driving my Jeep with the top down on a beautiful, fall day. I was listening to my favorite music. I was enjoying the ride.

Then I began to think about time—how much had passed, how little we have, and how I wish I could have had more of it with Chris. I desperately asked Chris to let me know if he could see me, if he could hear me. I looked around eagerly for his face thinking he might appear to me saying, "It's OK." I pulled off of the road into a wooded area, got out of the Jeep and bent over and cried. I leaned back and searched the sky for Chris's face. I sat down. I got up. I wandered around the woods. I cried so hard that the muscles in my face and in my stomach were aching. I spoke to Chris through sobs.

"I can't believe you're gone. I can't believe it. Why did this happen? "

I thought about Chris's personality and how active and optimistic he was. How could someone like that die? I just stood there in disbelief and wailed. I had a recurring thought that I've heard others express many times since then. How could someone so full of life die? How is that possible?

That day I couldn't shake the pain and the questioning. I built up a mountain of questions and had no answers. At least, I had no answers that made me feel better. The void grew. On other days I am able to cry for a few minutes privately in the car. That day I just couldn't stop. It was one of my hardest days because there was no relief. At the end of a full day of anger, sadness, confusion, and emptiness, I was left with two undeniable truths: My brother died, and I would never share the earth with him again. What an awful feeling!

That same day I pulled out my "Chris" file and read through the collection containing letters we wrote to each other, meaningful and also humorous clippings and quotations that Chris had gathered and kept, and some sympathy cards I received after Chris's accident.

One of the letters I wrote to Chris responded to the sadness he had expressed over the marriage of a girl he'd long adored. The letter tried to convince him not to worry—that he was the true catch and that he was too young to be hit so hard by the loss of a woman he hadn't seen in years. He was in college at the time. The last line of the letter said, "Just live and be alive, Chris."

I had a powerful rage inside. We didn't get to share a full life as brothers. Chris was no longer alive. That was the first day since Chris's death that I really felt out of control. It hit me suddenly on a beautiful day, and it hit me fiercely.

The acceptance of death and of grief was daunting because I knew that no matter what I did with my life, I would always have to face the reality. Chris won't be back. There is no equivalent for this intimidating feeling. I felt that I could not win. I felt helpless because I knew that I could not bring my brother back.

Chris was born in September 1967, and I was born in September 1969. When Chris died on December 5, 1994 he was twenty-seven years old. I was twenty-five. After a year had passed I began to think about an inevitable oddity. I would live longer than Chris lived. I would be older than my older brother. I had no specific feeling about it. I didn't know how to feel about it. I just thought about how unnatural it would be.

I turned twenty-seven in 1996, and in November,1996, I told my parents, "In twelve days I will have lived longer than Chris lived. I'll be older than him." On December 6, 1996, I was older than my older brother. It was a day that I had anticipated with a sour feeling in my stomach. I thought about it from every angle. It was not a day of outward displays of emotion. It was a hard day because I reflected on the meaning of the day. But there was no meaning. I was still alive. My life was continuing to progress. I had lived longer than Chris. Even now it is a strange concept to grasp.

It was a hard day because I didn't want it to come. There are several days like this. The first birthday, death date, holiday, and many other days are hard. The days come whether I want them to or not. The days may seem longer than others, but they are exactly the same in length. Distracting activities may help, but taking the time to look around and wonder why I feared the day (when it's not as bad as I thought it would be) can also help.

Every year on the anniversary of Chris's death I take the day off work and spend it with my parents. We talk about Chris. We look at pictures together and tell stories about him. We cry and laugh. We acknowledge the hardest day of all, the day we lost him.

CHAPTER FOURTEEN

A NEW YOU

Some people say that experiencing loss makes us reevaluate our priorities. I believe that. It was most evident to me in the days and weeks right after Chris's death. I spent hours contemplating the importance of various functions and actions. I thought about things that cause stress like car insurance, test scores, and bad haircuts. How much do these things matter? Shop for the best insurance and be satisfied. Prepare for tests and then create your world with your resources. Hair grows out. What is important? Family, friends, love, trust, and fun. These are the litanies of early grief.

I thought through conversations in which I may have not represented myself well. I decided that I was who I was at that time, and my true nature probably revealed itself in my facial expressions, hand movements, and tone of voice. Word choice is important, but intentions always win over semantics.

I realized that there is usually no need for worry. Most people manufacture their worries. In the 1950s novel <u>On the Road</u> one of the characters is riding in the back of a car. The people in the front seat are stressed out by their daily troubles. The character says, " They have worries, they're counting the miles, they're thinking about where to sleep tonight, how much money for gas, the weather, how they'll get there—and all the time they'll get there anyway, you see. But they need to worry and betray time with urgencies false and otherwise, purely anxious and whiny, their souls really won't be at peace unless they can latch on to an established and proven worry and having once found it they assume facial expressions to fit and go with it, which is, you see, unhappiness, and all the time it all flies by them and they know it and that too worries them no end." The challenge is to remember those early litanies on down the line.

After three years I drift into a busy life which hasn't much time for fresh thoughts. But there are days when I remember Chris's voice and the way he would brag about me to his friends. On those days I can think away the manufactured distractions of my life and focus on the simple truths. What's important is that we let people know how we feel, what we think, that we recognize each other's potential. If you take away the distractions, the self-imposed worries and mental obstacles, we all just want to be appreciated and to be able to share our appreciation with someone else.

Am I more sensitive now? I cry when I'm touched by a moment, and I rarely cried before. I'm not too embarrassed to have tears in front of a friend, but I am embarrassed about making noise when I cry. I tell my parents that I love them much more often than I did before. My dad and I hug much more often that we did before. Sometimes I watch my wife's three young cousins, all boys, and I almost cry for the hope that they'll be able to share long lives together. I wish that Chris and I could have lived our dreams. I cry for the future without him. The world is a different place without him, and I am a different person.

I am different now. I've learned to expect to feel different, to be treated differently at times, to behave differently, to say different things, to have new interests... I am not the same person I was before the death. I am a new me living in a new world. I don't take friends for granted any more. I appreciate simple gestures of kindness and feel deeply for others who are suffering a similar loss. There are new factors thrown into the equations of my life.

There is an occasional tension, a tension that is out of reach and irritating. I want it to go away. The smallest of decisions causes anxiety and hesitation. My parents ask, "How do you feel about doing _____ for Christmas this year?" I know exactly how I feel about it, but I must consider the feelings of my parents who are also grieving and struggling. Do I say that I want to do only what I want to do because it is all that I can do? Do I go along with their plans knowing that they want only the best for me? Where there was no tension before, now there is tension.

How many pictures should I display? What would be too much? Will people think it is strange to have too many pictures up? What do I do with Chris's shoes? What would he want me to do with them? There are new issues.

I received some money from my brother's life insurance. Should I feel guilty about the convenience of having it? How should I use it? What would he want me to do with it? Some people call it blood money, but I don't think of it that way. It is another gesture of generosity. The money is to be taken seriously and not handled foolishly, no matter how much it is. I invested it responsibly, so it will grow like a tree, slowly but steadily. Chris would appreciate that.

My parents ask, "Scott, how are you, really?" It makes sense for them to ask me. Before Chris died I would have thought it was weird for them to ask me that. I would have wondered what led them to believe that there was a reason to ask. Now I know why they ask. They ask because we, the three of us, are dealing with a different world. We are new people living in a new world. We are still bound by what we think is appropriate. We might want to stand outside in the rain staring into the sky or to read old letters and cry over lunch, but we do what we think is appropriate. We usually hold the energy inside, smothering our grief with inhibition. We let it out in small gasps and feel great relief afterwards. We should let it out in wide yawns.

There is a place I go. It is a place created by my father and my mother and their parents before them, a place where blood flows and pounds like a wild river. Currents rise and rush into the world of my body and carry with them the warmth of my memories and the strength of one hundred years. Deep inside those floods of youth, of dreams, of what I wish were here rushing over me, is a place I used to know and love. Below the bubbling surface of gushes of life is the place where my brother lives in my heart.

I dive deeply to that place when I am feeling especially strong. I dive through my old shame for tears and into myself. In the sunlight I tilt my head back and search the sky for his smile. At night in bed, I listen to the air for his voice, expecting a whisper, hoping, and knowing that what will really come is a restless sleep. I have photographs, stories, memories, and lessons learned. I have tears and smiles. I have within the rivers of my lifeblood the same seed that gave life to my brother, and in it I carry the will to live fully, the will that Chris displayed so well.

Our blood was the same, but only my blood pulses daily through the chambers of my heart. Only my lungs exchange this air for breath, and only this face can smile at a song. I am writing this book because there is too much fear in dealing with death, because I love my family, and mostly because this is the wooded path to my heart full of sunlight and shadows. I need to tell Chris that I love him one more time for everyone to hear.

I think of Chris's wink of life and gracious smile full of years. There is a struggle in me to help myself, and in so doing, a wish to help others who have lost the one whom they were sure they could not live without. I remember the things I thought about in the weeks after my sibling's death. I try to remember what is truly important to me. Remind myself that the little things don't matter so much. They don't matter enough to let them worry me. I am living through a traumatic experience and need time to adjust to the grief. I don't want to doubt myself. I made it through yesterday; I can make it through today. I might not want to run back to the gym or pick up the computer, but I can think about the kind of person I want to be, and be that person. I am a new me in a new world.

CHAPTER FIFTEEN

THE PROFESSONAL EAR

I watched a movie that dealt with the relationship between brothers and was reminded of how special my relationship was with Chris. I cried during the movie and thought about Chris's death and felt sorry for myself. The more I dwelled on his absence, the worse I felt. My stomach ached, and I was getting the chills. I was physically sick from depression. I just wanted to curl up into a ball and cry and be warm again. My head was pounding from the strain of crying, and I understood the intensity with which we can feel alone and lost. That was a hard day, and a restless night's sleep wasn't much of a remedy.

The bereaved are always walking along a canyon. I am focusing on footholds, trying to stay on stable ground. Some days I am able to look down into the canyon and appreciate where I am in my grief. On other days I fall and am frustrated by the struggle to get back to where I was. It feels like going backwards, like losing ground, but that is not what it is. When I fall into a short period of depression, it is just part of my survival. It takes work to climb out of it, but once I do so, I am back on the trail. I am enjoying the scenery once again.

Some people will feel helpless and become inactive. I've had days like that, and I've had weeks like that. Then I thought about Chris and the kind of person he was. I thought about the point of view we shared-- that life was to be lived to the fullest. We used to say that we would not merely exist, we would live. I guess we all have our own definition of what that means, but to me, it means working to accept the fact that the canyon is there. A fall is always one step away, but if I should fall, I know I have the strength within me to find my way back to where I was. If I remain lying on my back for too long, I am merely existing, taking up space and air. If I face the fear and face the future knowing the danger of what lies so near, I gain confidence and strength. I know I am able to survive. I choose to live my life.

After hitting the six -month mark and having several hard days, I thought about going to talk to a grief counselor. The company I work for had an Employee Assistance and Referral Service. They paid for three free visits for each member of an employee's family per year. The EARS program offered counseling for a wide range of personal problems, but I just wanted to vent a little. I wanted to talk to someone without having to think about what I was saying, without holding back. I had reached the point where the people around me seemed to have forgotten, and I was desperate. I felt totally hollow, and it bothered me. I have always been the kind of guy who just kept going. My emotional wound was still hurting, and I decided to seek some assistance.

I was nervous about calling a counselor, but I thought it was necessary. I called and set up an appointment. I was immediately proud of myself for taking action. When the time came to drive to the EARS office, my palms became cold and clammy. I was swallowing and yawning, and I just wanted it to be over so I could feel good about it. Sitting on the couch in the reception area was tough. My legs were bouncing, and I had to clear my throat to keep my voice steady. It was nerve-wracking. I worked myself up, psyching myself up so I wouldn't break down. I was determined not to cry, to show this counselor that I was tougher than most, that I was iron-willed. I realize now how foolish I was.

My counselor greeted me with a friendly smile and a firm handshake. I liked him immediately. We walked back to his little office, and I noticed that he was very relaxed. It helped me to relax a little. I took some deep breaths and sat on the couch directly across from him. He said, "Most people sit on the end of the couch or on the chair, but I just move over to face them. You're brave." We laughed. I told him what happened to my brother. He asked me some questions. I answered them. I talked, and he listened.

Fifty minutes went by too quickly. I wanted to keep talking, but I felt much better. It felt great to pour everything out. I was eager to set up another appointment. After learning first-hand how helpful it was, I had no more fear of the unknown. I told my parents that it was exactly what I needed.

I needed some help, and I asked for it. A counselor can help. There is absolutely nothing wrong or weird about visiting a professional. If nothing else, they will listen with an experienced ear. That alone is comforting. I started visiting the counselor six months after Chris died. I went once a week for few weeks, then twice a month, once a month, and eventually once or twice a year. It has helped me tremendously. I go whenever I feel that I need to talk. It has the same effect on me as attending church; I leave feeling much better than when I arrived.

All I know about depression is what it feels like. I learned to do what is best for me, and I believe that every moment is an opportunity. Why not take advantage of each of them? I learned to help myself by giving myself what I needed to survive. If I need a new and different job or a new hobby, I'll find one. If I need a friend, I'll call one. If I need to write a poem, I'll write one. If I want to talk to someone confidentially, I'll call a counselor. Time will work on some of the pain, but it will always be there, like a canyon one step away.

I think of a counselor as a guide, one who lets me know what to expect, one who has mapped out the trail along the canyon and has helped others complete the hike. The only drawback to a counselor is that he might never have been in the canyon. Sensing this need, my counselor suggested that I visit a group called The Compassionate Friends. He said there were surviving siblings that met there once a month just to talk about their experience. I decided to check it out.

I relived the whole self-imposed drama of sharing my grief with strangers. I drove to a church one night when the Sibling Group was supposed to meet. No one was there. I got a copy of The Compassionate Friends newsletter and called a name from the front page. A kind woman answered my questions about the discussion groups and told me where I could find a group that was more convenient. I showed up and thanked God afterwards that such a group existed. There is no substitute for sitting in a room full of people who understand what you are going through.

The Sibling Group is a safe place to share. Tears are allowed as well as guilt- free smiles. Most people never hear about the groups like Compassionate Friends until they lose a child or a sibling, but it is a great organization. In the Sibling Group understanding comes easily. Surviving siblings share stories and experiences, ask questions, and sometimes just listen and observe. We all have days when we don't feel like talking. In the sibling group I was welcome to talk, listen, cry, etc. It was comforting.

We talked about how we adjusted, how others reacted to the news when they first heard it, how soon we should tell a girlfriend or boyfriend about our grief, how we dealt with court scenes, how we struggled with the image of the car accident, how our parents handled their grief, and how our other siblings handled their grief. We recognized the birthdays and the anniversaries of death dates of our deceased siblings. We called each other when we needed to talk between meetings. We e-mailed each other. We developed a small network of friends who have experienced what we have experienced, and we can count on each other to understand.

The Sibling Group goes like this. We sit in a circle and talk. No one is trained to counsel or to be a good listener, but it is very therapeutic. I found out about the Compassionate Friends through my counselor, and the combination of seeking some counseling and attending a grief support group has made the difference for me.

My counselor has been great for me, and I call him when I need to talk. He says I can call anytime, even if I just need to cry over the phone. He also suggests having a friend who says I can call even if I just need to cry over the phone. It was hard to approach a friend about this, but I did and was pleased with the response. I have never done it, but it's nice to know I can if I need to.

My counselor is a resource. He gives me ideas and responds to my questions. He does not cost too much. He does not examine me like a patient. He just listens to me and responds appropriately. For me it isn't a medical situation; it's an emotional situation. He helps me understand some of the predictable aspects of bereavement, and I help him get to know me. Now that he knows a lot about me, he can counsel me more effectively.

I had read several tips about going to counseling. "It is important that you choose your counselor. A company insurance plan may provide several options, but you should ask about the counselors and decide who will be best for you. If you are young but will be in counseling without your parents, then they don't need to make the decision for you. Ask them if you can choose. If you don't like the way you are treated, make a change. You determine the value of your counseling experience." I was glad that I got a good one.

I used to be self-conscious talking about counseling because I didn't want people to think that something was wrong with me. I wanted them to think that I could handle everything. I could handle everything, but I could handle it all much better with a little guidance. The counselor helps to make some sense out of the chaos in my mind. There is nothing wrong with seeing a counselor. It does not mean that something is wrong with me. It just means that I have the strength to seek help. Trust me. It feels good to release the emotions that are bottled up inside. I learned that it's okay to ask for help.

A counselor or a psychologist won't judge and should be a wonderful listener. A bereavement group is less confrontational because there is no pressure to speak. I benefited from both. The sooner I learned to express my grief, the better off I was.

CHAPTER SIXTEEN

ACCEPTANCE

Missing Chris is as much a part of my life as thinking is a part of my life. I think of him and miss him frequently every day. I keep a book of daily reflections on grief in my desk at work, and the bookmark in it is a photograph of Chris. Sometimes I open the book and just look at Chris's face. I think about his charm, his vulnerability, his sense of adventure and spontaneity, his intelligence, and on and on. Most of all I think about his love for our family. Girls that Chris dated used to pull me aside and tell me how much Chris loved me, how proud he was of me, and how much he said he owed to our parents for what they taught him of love and respect and decency.

I wish I had videos of him and recordings of his voice, but I don't. Missing Chris, missing the life we had together is part of who I am. I say this because I live a positive life, and I am generally a happy person. I have one hand in happiness, the memories we made together, and one hand in isolation, the world without my brother. I constantly push and pull in an attempt to firmly remember yet triumphantly live a positive life. It is possible to feel the pain, to wish something else had happened, to grieve healthily without giving up on life. Chris and I had conversations about death, and he would say that if he ever died before me that I should still seek out my life and have fun.

The world is a different place. I am a different person.

Death prompts an evaluation of priorities. It reminds me of the things I take for granted. It forces me to weigh the values that I assign to things in my life. I look at my jobs, my relationships, my dreams, and myself. I contemplate my future and try to store my past. I know that my life will be different.

Chris is gone. Sometimes things don't come with a reason. I can't explain in cosmic terms why Chris died. I have the choice to live in the whys and what ifs and always be miserable or to acknowledge the positive contribution that my brother made to my life by giving equally of myself and making the world a better place. It's not all about religion or psychology. It's about accepting my grief and adjusting my stance so that I can continue my life while carrying it.

Over time my body adjusts. Muscles develop and mental attitudes improve. I strengthen and grow. After daily practice over a period of time determined by me, I can carry it well. The point is not to dwell on the past but to appreciate it and make the most of the present from what I learned in the past.

When I was in elementary school Chris had a saying that annoyed me greatly. If I complained or made excuses about something like losing a soccer game, Chris said, "Life is hard." He said the sooner we accept the fact that life is hard, the better prepared we are for its challenges and opportunities. He would also respond to my gripes with, "Who said life was fair?" He taught me early on that life is not balanced and fair. Life is what I make of it. I'm thankful for my big brother's teaching. Now I know the true value of his words.

All who have lost brothers, sisters, children, parents, grandparents, and friends have learned that life is hard. I deal with the question of fairness in moments of despair. Through it all, nothing I ask and nothing I say can change where I am now. And knowing that life can be hard and unfair prepares me for the rest of my life. Where others may be hurt, shocked, and discouraged by setbacks and tragedies, I now understand that these tragedies are a part of my life. I know that I am vulnerable. I know that my world may be flipped inside out at any moment. I may be knocked down, but I continue to get back up. Perhaps I also know the depth of love more completely.

It is easy to think that I always felt the excitement of life when Chris was alive. It is easy to convince myself that, if he were still alive, my life would be completely satisfying. I would have no worries. Some part of me knows that that is not true, but most of me also knows that without my brother on it, this world is a lonelier place. My father, my mother, and I agree that the grief is with us every day—that there are days when we don't want to go to work. There are moments when it seems like too much to handle. We also agree that we are lucky. We had in our lives a person whom we loved and cherished and who loved and cherished us for twenty-seven years. We are lucky to have shared a large part of our lives with such a wonderful person. Our only logical choice now is to do our best to create happiness again.

AFTERWORD

BRIDGING THE COMMUNICATION GAP

After going to the Sibling Group for over a year I was asked to be a co-leader of the group. I was not sure if I could help anyone, but I knew that I could get a discussion going and show newly bereaved siblings that they could live through the overwhelming grief. Before each monthly meeting I would set aside some time to think about important and relevant issues that we should talk about. I thought about the descriptions that I had heard many times from many different people in the group, and I recognized a large communication gap between bereaved parents and their surviving siblings.

-Recognizing the Gap-

The first few times I went to the Compassionate Friends' meetings, there weren't enough siblings to have a sibling group, so I sat in on the parents' group. They asked, "Why doesn't my son talk to me?"

I said, "I can't speak for anyone but myself, but I have ideas. Maybe he doesn't know what to say because he doesn't know how to put his feelings into words." I thought to myself, siblings see that their parents are overwhelmed with grief and do not want to add to the burden. Some parents are so consumed with their own grief that they temporarily lose their ability to empathize. They still have sincere concern but must focus on themselves to get by.

The bereaved parents in the group asked, "Do you feel like you are taking care of your parents?"

I said, " The week or two after Chris's death I did. I still worry about them, but I know that they have to grieve."

"Are you angry at your brother for leaving you behind?

" I said, "No. I don't understand that. It just does not relate to me. If I felt that he was behaving recklessly and carelessly, I might wish that he were more cautious, but I know he did not make a decision to die. I could never be mad at him for something that was not his choice."

During the discussion I realized that the parents were focusing on me. Their questions were directed to me instead of to each other. When they spoke, I could sense the eyes of the others on me, searching for my reaction. They were intensely curious about my thoughts and feelings as a surviving sibling. They wanted to know what my experience was like.

-The Survey-

When I thought about those questions and about the statements I heard often in the sibling group, I came up with an idea. I brought it up at the planning meeting for our chapter. "What if we did a survey of bereaved parents and a survey of surviving siblings, compiled the responses, and shared the results with each group? We could share the parent survey with the siblings and share the sibling survey with the parents. We could really learn something." Everyone agreed that it would be worthwhile.

The webmasters for the Atlanta Chapter of The

Compassionate Friends posted the parent survey on the T.C.F. website, and the responses were e-mailed directly to my home computer. Parents from all over the world filled out the survey, and I spent hours and hours reading through them, feeling for the bereaved parents. The responses touched my heart. I am more sensitive to other's loss because of my own loss. I know what it feels like. I appreciated the effort that parents made to answer personal questions openly.

I found a website called Juliesplace for young, surviving siblings, and asked the woman who created the site if she would post the sibling survey on her site. She and I sent messages back and forth for a few weeks, clarifying what we wanted to do and why. She lost her sister and had created the site for other surviving siblings, so she was curious to see if we would get any responses. Once the survey was on her site, the responses started coming in. We got so many responses that I asked her to take it off of her site. I said I just could not read them all if they kept coming so fast. My printer was hot, and I had stacks of sibling responses.

The combination of my role in the sibling group and my exposure to all of the survey responses taught me plenty. The parents called out for communication with their surviving children, and the children said they did not understand their parents' behavior. There is a large communication gap between bereaved parents and surviving siblings. I read about children who don't talk to their parents about the grief, and I read about parents who would not allow their children to discuss their deceased sibling. I listened as other siblings talked about competitive grief, and I heard them describe the phone calls from their parents as excruciating and depressing. I was touched by stories of married couples growing closer through their grief and understanding of couples who could no longer live together. Siblings in the group sometimes described their parents as being consumed by their grief, while parents wrote about the concern that their surviving children did not grieve enough. The underlying wish was for better communication.

-Competitive Grief-

Sometimes surviving siblings get caught up in gauging their grief against the grief of others. One bereaved sibling put it this way, "My mother said that I have no idea how bad her pain is, but I think she has it easier than me. She and dad have each other to talk to, to cry with, and to share memories. She spent half of her life with my sister, but I spent my whole life with her until two months ago. Now I am an only child. It is much tougher on me."

This girl's mother says to her, "I carried your sister inside of my body for nine months while she developed and grew. I breast fed her and wiped her behind. I picked her up when she fell down and taught her about love and kindness. Everything I did, I did it for you two girls. When she died, I died with her." The mother and daughter quoted above often argue about who hurts the most. Each wants the other to sympathize, but both feel neglected, so they won't give in. They have arguments over the phone that increase the growing distance between them. A twenty-year old male surviving sibling said his mother "feels like she is the sole owner of the grief, that what she feels is so much more than what I could feel." This is competitive grief.

It is possible to be in the middle of a large crowd and still feel lonely. I think about human nature, about the world inside of myself. My emotions can be in absolute opposition to the nature of my environment. I've been in terrible moods on beautiful days and great moods on nasty days.

I've heard of people feeling weak in their strongest moments. I know that my will is stronger than circumstance. There is a dangerous game that tough guys play. Two guys put their forearms together and place a burning cigarette in the valley formed between their arms. The guy who moves his arm away first loses the game. Afterwards both guys are burnt, in pain and wondering what the point was. Neither proves anything valuable. We can try to ignore the pain, but it will hurt us more, and competing with pain is a lose-lose situation.

Each of us grieves individually, whether we are alone in life, living with our families or surrounded by hordes of close friends. Competing with grief is a destructive way to grieve. When I am struggling to do the best I can, I don't want to add stress and conflict to the mix. Sometimes I feel that no one could possibly feel as badly as I do. It is impossible to prove that one person's grief is more intense than someone else's grief. At a time when family and friendships are so important, competing with grief can make matters tougher. Parents have hard days, and surviving siblings have hard days. Each of us deals with our grief in our own private way.

How can I measure the depth of an abyss? And if I could measure it's depth, what would I do with the information? Would it be beneficial to my life? Once I'm in the abyss, I just want to find my way out of it. I want to survive.

-Family Redefinition-

Death may add tension to family relationships. Surviving siblings are often disappointed in their parents, wanting them to continue to be the strong, optimistic people they've always been. They say things like, "My mom was always so strong. She held us together whenever times were hard, but now she spends all day in bed. She doesn't even seem interested in the future of our family." I want my parents to be invincible, to maintain the image I created of them when I was young. I want them to persevere, to say, "We can live through anything." Some children grow up with selfless parents who always put their children before themselves. When a parent loses a child, the pain and introspection may prevent the parent from continuing to give the expected attention to the child. Bereaved parents need time to grieve, just as surviving siblings need time to grieve.

The point is that surviving the death of a brother or sister is different for each survivor, regardless of the circumstances surrounding the death, because people are different. The roles that we play in relation to other people's lives are complex. Father, mother, brother, sister, cousin, girlfriend, buddy—each plays an individual role in the life of the other. Maybe none of them can fully be understood or defined. Just as two siblings may grieve differently, one weeping openly and the other refusing to discuss the matter, two parents grieve differently. Even though they have each other, each could be acting and reacting in totally different ways while occupying the same space.

If they're married, they are sharing a house, but do they feel secure? Do they feel alone, as I sometimes do, even though they are not alone? Parents can feel as siblings do. Siblings can feel as parents do. When a father remembers a special moment shared with his child, he can feel a sense of connection and a sense of loss. He can cry inside for the voice of his child and pray at night to remember the laughter. Siblings can remember when they helped their sibling through a rough time, when they protected or supported their sibling. They might have felt like they were parenting a child during those times. Surviving siblings say, "We felt a special bond that no one else will understand." True. Parents say, "There is nothing like losing a child. You couldn't possibly imagine." Also true.

When parents are taking the necessary time to grieve, their surviving child may convince himself that his parents don't care about him. He might think that they loved his deceased sister more than him or that they wish he was the one to go instead. I have heard siblings express these thoughts in the sibling discussion group. When parents stop giving the attention and the sympathy that a child has grown accustomed to, sometimes the child takes it personally and thinks it may be because of something he did or didn't do. This is another reason why some surviving siblings do not talk with their parents about their grief. I've heard siblings say, "They are too wrapped up in their own grief to have to worry about mine. I don't want to add anything to the burden they already carry. It's time for me to be an adult and handle my own problems." Then this message turns into an emotional one. "They only talk about my (deceased) sister. They have pictures of her on their desks at work and no pictures of me. She is all they talk about. It's like they wish it were me instead of her." This is when the tears begin to flow.

Sometimes, even if bereaved parents show plenty of concern and make an effort to be available to their surviving child, the child still won't talk to them. "I know that my parents are depressed, and I want them to think that I am doing fine. It will be the only thing that they don't have to worry about." In the parent survey I asked the question, "What is the difference between the first few weeks or months and the way you feel now?" Most parents said that they felt total shock at first. They were numb and could not believe that their child had died. They were empty and felt angry, sometimes at God. They were unable to let go and had trouble concentrating and sleeping. A few parents mentioned that they wanted to kill themselves because they felt that their life was over. The grief was just too much, so much that they neglected surviving children. Several parents described a lack of interest in life and a paralyzed feeling. The overwhelming cause of all of these feelings was the inability to cope with the absence of their child.

After a few years they said the reality has sunk in—they know that this is real. There is still crying but less crying. Emotions are still intense, but they have learned to live with the grief. Time helped. They can smile without feeling guilty and think of tomorrow again, but the loss is a major part of their lives. In some cases Prozac assisted in the effort to live a positive life. Sometimes they still feel withdrawn and lost. Most bereaved parents said that they still miss their child greatly, but that they have learned to live with the grief.

When I asked about changes in surviving children, the most common answer was that the surviving children do not talk about it. They don't acknowledge the loss or confirm their love for their deceased brother or sister. They tend to be guarded and seem to keep themselves distant. Many surviving children become angry, lonely, and less confident. They seem lost. These descriptions are similar to siblings' descriptions of their parents, with one exception. Siblings usually feel that their parents talk about their sibling too much, making the conversation forced and unnatural.

An almost equal number of surviving children are much more sensitive to their parents' needs. They are much stronger and more mature than they were before their sibling's death. The relationship between the parents and surviving children grows stronger. They say, "I love you," more often than they did before. Some surviving children have grief- related illnesses. With this much pain and emotion it is easy to see how communication is affected.

-Opening Up-

I posed the following question to bereaved parents in the survey: If you were giving advice to grieving children about the best way to interact positively with bereaved parents, what would you tell them? The answers in their words-- Share your feelings. Talk about it. Acknowledge our loss. We need to know that you still miss and love your sibling. Have patience with us. Let us cry. Don't rush us. Understand the depth of the loss that we feel and know that we love you. We miss your sibling but don't love him/her more than we love you. You are a different person and just as important to us. Remember that we still have each other and that we should make the most of our time together.

-Husbands and Wives-

To make matters more complicated there are role changes within the family such as the youngest child becoming the only child or the middle child becoming the oldest child. And on top of the distance that may be created between parents and their surviving children, there is a distance between husbands and wives. In reading the survey responses I was interested in the answers to the question, "How has your marital relationship been affected?" The most common answer was that the relationship has grown stronger. Parents were angry at first , had lost their focus on life, and sometimes blamed each other unnecessarily. Loving partners learned each other's differences, shared their feelings with each other, and supported each other. One person said, "We've shared joy. We've shared sorrow, but most of all we've shared love. And that love has held us together." There is a myth that over fifty percent of bereaved parents get divorced.

Less than ten percent of the parents who responded to the survey were divorced after the death of their child. Problems were caused when husbands tried to fix or solve the situation. Sometimes the couple did not know how to comfort each other and lacked the energy for physical contact. Several of the parents who responded were not married when their child passed away. The couples who stayed together had a few things in common. They gave each other room to grieve privately and respected each other's boundaries. They learned when to comfort and when to be quiet. They expressed their grief openly and admitted that they could not fix it. They communicated.

This seemed to be the most personal of all the questions in the survey. The couples who said that their relationship is closer now also described the hard times and the struggle to share their grief. One parent thought that this subject might not be appropriate for siblings, but I think it is important for surviving siblings to view the grief of their parents as the grief of individuals—to understand that we all grieve differently.

When there are two or more surviving siblings, the dynamics of their relationship seem to mirror that of a marriage. Sometimes they communicate very well and their bond grows stronger. They share their pain. Sometimes they do not discuss the death, and one of them resents the lack of compassion that is displayed by the other. The distance grows between them, and they turn to their friends for support. I've seen both of these dynamics in action in the sibling discussion group.

-Friends-

Responses from the sibling survey and the parents' survey were similar to the question, "How have your friends responded to your loss?" There were two common responses. The first was that friends were very supportive. They were not afraid to talk about their friend's loss and would call and leave phone messages saying things like, "I was thinking of your brother today, and I really miss seeing his smile." When long-term friendships were stressed, the relationships recovered when the stress was discussed. Many bereaved parents noted the importance of telling their friends how to help. Friends often volunteered to help but did not really know what to do, so telling them how to help was rewarding.

The second answer was that friends didn't know what to say. They said nothing, avoided the subject, and eventually quit calling. One person said, "Some friends are great friends, and some are no longer friends." Siblings often say that kids at school act as if grief is contagious by staying away from them. Knowing that some friends have the best intentions but do not know what to say, I asked this question, "What do people say that helps you continue to live a positive life?"

Many parents responded by saying that there was nothing anyone could say to help them, but the most helpful statement that friends offered to parents were ,"You will see your child again." Siblings enjoyed hearing their friends tell stories of their deceased sibling. Helpful statements that were listed included the following: "We are thinking of you. I am sorry about your loss. We love you and are here for you when you need us. It was not your fault. You were a good parent or you and your brother were so close." Getting more specific, I asked bereaved parents to list what helped them the most. Here is a breakdown of their responses.

The Compassionate Friends support group	28%
Friends	20%
Religious faith/Pastor	12%

Books	9%
Spouse	7%
Counseling/Therapy	7%
Writing/Reading Poetry	6%
Visits from child's friends	5%
Surviving children	3%
Websites	1%
Dreams about child	1%
Prozac	1%

Notice that surviving siblings were only mentioned in three percent of the responses to that question—proof of the communication gap. No one is to blame. It is just a simple fact that bereaved parents and surviving siblings are consumed by their own grief. It's hard to help someone else when you can barely help yourself. While parents and their surviving children may not support each other in the beginning of this long journey, their existence alone may be comforting at that time. Even when I wasn't volunteering any information about my feelings to my parents, I gained a sense of security by knowing that they were around. And I know they needed confirmation that I was around because the boundaries of possibility were stretched.

We needed to make sure that we were all still there, together, still alive. Only people who have lived through this experience can fully understand what it means to question existence. Once we were able to focus outside of ourselves, we began to share our concerns with each other. This is when some parents realize that their surviving children are not opening up to them. The newly bereaved parent might think that her child is not grieving fully or is not expressing his grief, when in fact her son is having lengthy conversations with friends about his feelings.

-What Kids Want-

There are many self-created worries that come into play, including the feelings of guilt over not being able to "be there" for other members of the family at certain times. The surviving siblings whom I have known through the discussion group cared deeply for their parents but did not always want to grieve with them. They had their own reasons including the ones mentioned previously.

Surviving children talk with their parents more when their parents say, "We are here for you. We don't expect you to replace your sister. We love you for who you are, and we want to be able to talk with you about her. We don't expect you to live her life or try to fill the gap. We just want you to know that we want you to talk about what you're going through. We don't need to be protected." When asked what parents could do to help bridge the communication gap, one young surviving sibling said, "Pushing doesn't work. Don't try to read our minds or make assumptions. Don't compare grief. Just be there."

A sure way for bereaved parents to cut off the communication from their surviving child is to separate the surviving child from the deceased child by saying that the deceased sibling's name should not be mentioned again. Siblings universally resent this way of approaching grief. Similar tactics involve parents who will not allow surviving siblings to go into their deceased sister's room or wear her clothes or perfume. I love to wear my brother's old clothes. I have photos of him wearing the clothes, and it helps me feel close to him. If my parents tried to deny me that simple salve, I would not understand it.

The best piece of advice for parents, siblings, friends, and relatives comes from the young man's advice to parents. Just be there.

Photograph by Holly Painter

About the author . . . .

Scott Mastley lives in Georgia with his
wife and daughter and is involved with
The Village Writers Group in Decatur,
Georgia.

YES, I want to help surviving siblings and those who love them! Please send _____ copies of <u>Surviving a Sibling</u> at $12.95 each plus $3 per book shipping. Canadian orders must be accompanied by a postal money order in U.S. funds and add another $3 per book shipping.

____ I am ordering five or more copies of <u>Surviving a Sibling</u>. Please reduce the price to $10.00 each plus $3 per book shipping.

Name_____

Phone_____

Company_____

Address_____

City/State/Zip_____

____ My check is enclosed.

____ Bill my ____ Visa ____ Mastercard

Acct#_____ Exp. _____

Signature _____

Here's my check or money order made out to The Box Press for $_____.

Mail to:
The Box Press
P.O. Box 1925
Suwanee, GA 30024-0975